Tales from the Red Pump

~~~ 130 Years of Northland Wisconsin Family Adventures ~~~

Thomas Wayne King

Tales from the Red Pump
~~ 130 Years of Northland Wisconsin Family Adventures ~~

Third Edition   August 18, 2016

Front cover pump photo by Thomas Wayne King.   Back cover snow art photo by Debra Raye King.
Back cover bio portrait by JoAnn Jardine.

The author is solely responsible for contents of this book.

My earlier renderings of some *Tales* appeared under various titles in other publications. >>Tales which appeared in the *Superior Daily Telegram*, Superior, Wisconsin, include: *A Smart Dog; Adam's Elephant; Blue Moon, Ricky Raccoon, and UNO; Do Over; Explorations in the Park; For Molly; Giants through Adult Eyes; Growing up with Pines; Hankadookadee and the Worm Bus; If You Had Just One Day; Land of Giants; Lyla and Syd...those other Relatives; Moccasin Mike Road, Melba Toast, and MacGyver; On By; Puppy Days Are Here Again; Skateboarding to Retirement; Sounds Like Spring; Thanks...for the Failure?; To Check the Trail; Toasted Science; What Party Was That?;* and *Winter Love.* >>*Blue Moon, Ricky Raccoon, and UNO* and *To Check the Trail* appeared in *The North Star*, magazine of the North Country Trail Association, Lowell, Michigan. >>*Adam's Elephant* appeared in *The Country Today* newspaper, Eau Claire, Wisconsin. >>*A Smart Dog; Blue Moon, Ricky Raccoon, and UNO; Explorations in the Park; Giants through Adult Eyes; Growing up with Pines; Hankadookadee and the Worm Bus; Land of Giants;* and *To Check the Trail* appeared on the St. Croix Riverfest 2008 website in the "Shared Words" section.

Library of Congress Cataloging-in-Publication Data

ISBN 978-0-578-04214-5

TALES

History is often told best in the small, simple stories. These forty *Tales from the Red Pump* tell of daily Northland life. Nothing grandiose at all, just life. Tales collected here recall glimpses of family and natural history, as well as views of our changing northwestern Wisconsin environment over more than 130 years of transition, from around 1880 to present. Each story can stand alone, or may be understood as part of a more comprehensive, detailed record of true northern, rural Wisconsin life, family events, and our natural world. *Tales from the Red Pump* may be read in any order.

Before Our Tales Begin

Preface and Acknowledgments

Our family, now and before me, made this book possible. You will read more about them beginning on the next page. My intense gratitude and apologies go to my wife, Debra, sons Seth and Adam, and daughter-in-law Lindsey, for the reclusive hours I have spent researching and writing this first in my trilogy collection of *Tales*. Additionally, I am grateful to them for the draft versions they have critiqued and endured. Their love, patience, and tolerance ultimately made this book a reality, lifting it above my intangible dream.

Tales from the Red Pump covers 130 years of family northland Wisconsin history, told in brief story snapshots. My Tales recounted here are actual family lore and events, represented as accurately as my memory is capable. All errors are mine. All credit goes to my extended Favell and King families for living such interesting, adventurous pioneering lives, and for passing on to me their supporting documents and the abilities and persistence to recap a bit of their stories for the ages. As I finish this book of real Tales about family and environment, I know that more adventures and cast await for our future northland stories. We plan to live many more Tales. And hopefully, maybe in a few years, I will have energy and time to write them down as well.

Tales from the Red Pump is dedicated to my grandmother, Inga, and my sister, Karen, both of whom I knew only in part. Inga and Karen were women of exceptional insights and abilities. Neither was well understood by others, and I wish I could have known and appreciated them more. I am grateful to them for their written words and music, and their humbling, poignant life stories of quiet tenacity.

Thank you, my family. This is for you. Enjoy and remember your *Tales*, and pass them on. Real history resides in the small stories of life.

Thomas Wayne King
Solon Springs, Wisconsin
January 28, 2009

Red Pump Beginnings

Can one place hold all your dreams? I believe it can. The Red Pump marks that place for me.

The Red Pump is a worn, upright cast-iron hand pump we bolted to our water well here years ago in Solon Springs. This humble monument is my center of the world. It marks the focus of where over five generations of our family have lived, learned, and played through adventures, joys, challenges, and tragedies. It is where I have grown to know much about being a son, brother, husband, father, a man. It anchors the one place where I know I can thrive the rest of my days. The Red Pump, and this land it secures, compose the stable, certain base from which I draw strength to leave and courage to return, always.

The Red Pump took residence here recently in the human history of this land. My father found the well-used pump at a nearby rural thrift store, and paid five dollars for it. The pump was a ragged, barn-red color when Dad bought it in spring, 1973. Shortly after he hauled it here, we bolted it to our newly drilled well in our small clearing in this old forest. Our deep well, along with our cherished pump, became the heart of this five-acre remnant of our family's original homestead from the post-Civil-War 1800s.

A few years later, we repainted our new-old pump a bright *glossy* red. Ever since, it has been "The Red Pump". Stories and reflections in this book diverge from this central, solid cast-iron catalyst of adventure and life learning; this one place, one symbol of continuity so important.

For over 130 years, our family felt the power and attraction of this special forest haven in the Upper St. Croix Lake basin of northwestern Wisconsin; our great grandparents, grandparents, and parents have all engaged in demanding, active lives here. My wife, our sons, and I also learned its draw. We appreciate this unique site more fully as we grow wiser. There is much to tell.

The Red Pump has become the heart of our homestead. Along with our compact living quarters in the midst of this mature, serene forest, the Red Pump also represents the heart of the north. It reminds us daily of the permanence of this place, the power of this climate, and the tenacity of all who live here. The Red Pump and its stories link to the northland Wisconsin heartbeat we have known in our lives for so many years, and are atop a deep reservoir of tales radiating from our unique homestead in an old forest.

This first offering of *Tales from the Red Pump* is only a beginning. There will be more.

If You Had Just One Day…

We moved back to Solon Springs permanently in 2004, to our small home in this old forest clearing. We had been gone too long. Every day now, we live, work, and play near the Red Pump. I am looking at it as I write.

Life here has become slower paced for me. At last I have time and opportunity here, after all these years of not truly knowing my origins or family's stories on both sides, to at least begin the involved, detailed process of going through boxes of family pictures, letters, and other memorabilia. It has been a time of diligent reacquaintance with my parents and older sister, who are now all deceased, and also of getting to know my grandparents and great grandparents whom, with one exception, I never met.

My view of life, the world, and of them, has changed so much. How wonderful to see Mom and Dad, even my grandparents and great grandparents, in long-stored pictures as teenagers, and to read some of their goofy personal letters and cards. They were young once, as I was, and seem so familiar. I never knew.

Sweating in our barn attic, as I sort through dusty boxes, is an adventure I had not imagined prior to our move back here. When I have time, I view and handle items, indeed treasures, some recent, some from long ago. It is much like entering a personal, family time machine. I see pictures and read of births, graduations, new jobs, lost jobs, and also of illnesses and deaths, of triumphs and tragic family losses, especially in way too many wars. It is quite a roller-coaster ride each time I look through things, learning more about these people of whom I know so little. They are becoming more real to me.

Some days, I find my exploration to be wonderful and exhilarating. Other days, as I read letters and documents of challenges, disappointments, and sorrows they all endured, through some gracefully long and some searingly short lives, I find it deeply humbling. It is an honor indeed to be among the latest in the family succession of those who lived their fullness of life here.

As I look through more things, my thoughts wander. I have come up with an interesting thought experiment. You may wish to try it: Imagine for one day of your choosing, just 24 hours, you, your parents, your grandparents, your great grandparents, and your great-greats as far back as you want (as well as your own children and your siblings, if you wish), can all be together -- and that you will all be the *same* age. What age will all of you be? What setting will you be in? What will you say and do? And why, for all of those?

This imagined scenario is interesting to work through. We can only wish it could happen, but it has caused me to examine relationships among and to long for interaction with relatives I have never known. It has also caused me to think in a more focused way about past family, whose lives and experiences have allowed my family today and me to be as we are.

Think about it. If you had just one day…

Blue Moon, Ricky Raccoon, and Uno

June 1981. Son Adam was about 2 years old. He and I needed an adventure together. Younger son, Seth, was not quite a year old, and needed time alone with Mom. So Adam and I packed his booster seat in the car, put in our hiking boots, camping gear, and some food, and headed for Lake St. Croix in Solon Springs, WI. It was just father and son, our first overnight camping adventure together, and Adam's first time away from Debbi, home, and little brother for more than a few hours.

We older King guys were heading out.

We drove south from Superior to our camping spot near Lake St. Croix to pitch our tent, hike the ancient portage trails, swim, build a campfire, and just have fun. By the way, camping or trail hiking or lake swimming or having a forest campfire with a not-quite-two-year-old may not involve the standard definitions we usually hold for these activities. Nonetheless, we were off to have our first just-guys adventure together, and were enjoying each other's company in the car.

As we drove south on Highway 53, I tuned the radio to an oldies station. The doo-wop song "Blue Moon" was playing. Adam and I bounced on down the road to it. I sang along, and he listened. After the song ended, I continued to sing "Blue Blue Blue Moon, dip di-dip di-dip…"

I was lost in my doo-wop world when Adam cut in. Using his most severe two-year old voice, he chirped, "Stop that Music!" He jolted me back to semi reality, and we drove on to Solon Springs, only *listening* to the radio.

As we neared our camping spot on a village back road, we saw a large raccoon cross in front of us. I slowed the car as we watched him amble into the woods where we would camp. I believe that was the first larger wild animal Adam had ever seen.

The two-year-old voice asked, "Who is that?" Interesting how Adam said "Who" not "What." That is how we have always thought of other critters.

Picking up on his cue, I responded, "That's Ricky Raccoon."

"Where's he going?" came the little voice again.

"He's going into the woods trails to visit his friend Malcolm Mole." I posed. That seemed to cover the matter.

When we set up our campsite, Adam became interested in the tall red farm pump we used to get our water. He had seen it before, but now the pump captured his full attention, although it was still too big and took too much strength for him to use at his small size. Nonetheless, he was fascinated by the motion and sound of the pump, and the flood of clear, cold, deep Solon Springs water it delivered each time I filled our buckets for cooking and washing. Our campout was great. We hiked to near exhaustion, and packed up the next afternoon to go home.

As we drove back to Superior the next day, I again started singing "Blue Blue Blue Moon..." Adam quickly gave me a sharp sideways glance, and in a playful way, said, "Stop that music!" I got the point.

Then Adam asked me to tell him a story. I made up this one as we drove home. It became a favorite of our young sons, and was retold by Mom and Dad at hundreds of bed times, and for years on every camping trip to Solon Springs:

6

Ricky Raccoon and Malcolm Mole were playing in the forest at Kingswood, where we camp. They got really thirsty, and tried to work our pump to get a drink. Ricky, the bigger animal, hopped up on the pump handle. He went down-and-up, down-and-up, down-and-up, down-and-up many times, but the water wouldn't pour out of the spout.

Ricky said "Malcolm, can you crawl down this pump spout, and see what's wrong?"

Malcolm called, "OK!" and he crawled into the pump. Inside, he found leaves and sticks had blown in during a storm. They blocked the water.

Malcolm Mole pulled the sticks and leaves out of the spout. He dropped them on the ground. Then he yelled "OK, Ricky!"

Ricky pushed the handle down-and-up, down-and-up, down-and-up, down-and-up -- and water gushed out of the pump.

Ricky Raccoon and Malcolm Mole got a good drink. They were very happy.

Epilogue: Over the next few years, as our preschool boys learned colors and numbers, and how to play with us and with each other, we would often enjoy the simple family game "UNO", with numbered, multi-colored cards. The rules say when you have your last card, you must yell "Uno!" so the other players know you are down to one card. Whenever I got a final card that was blue, I would sing "Blue Blue Blue Uno, dip, di-dip, di-dip…" and so on, in my best doo-wop voice.

Until Adam was about age five or so, with a twinkle in his eye over our inside joke, he would immediately say, "Stop that Music!" and give me that sideways glance he used on our first camping trip. It became a running joke between us and lasted for several years, until his father matured.

We built our permanent, little always-camping-out home at that same forest campsite in 2002, and walk by our Red Pump many times every day now. It is part of our lives. We think now of Dr. Adam, medical pediatrics resident, immersed in his distant, demanding urban life, and of those quiet, simple St. Croix summer adventures we had so many years ago. The Red Pump is a good reminder.

A Smart Dog

-- By Angela Haste Favell, circa 1893 --

Some years ago we were living on Upper Lake St. Croix at Solon Springs, Wisconsin, where we had a partly wooded ten-acre tract. On this we built a barn and converted most of the space into pasture for two cows. A friend gave us a puppy, half collie and half shepherd, that grew into a very intelligent and useful dog.

Going with his master to the milking was a chore our Jack greatly enjoyed and never would miss. He would drive up the cows, wait until milking was over, then return home carrying whatever article his master might entrust to him. Only one thing he enjoyed more than this milking trip. That was to hunt rabbits with our son who came from the city week-ends.

One Saturday after an early supper our son got out his gun and said to the dog, "Jack, bring my hunting boots and we will get a rabbit." Jack acted a little excited but confused for a moment. Then, instead of going right to the closet for the boots as he had done so many times before, he bolted out the kitchen door and ran up the hill toward the pasture. We were still puzzling over his unusual conduct when suddenly he reappeared, ran to the closet, brought out the boots and deposited them at our son's feet, thus announcing his readiness for the hunt.

Shortly after the hunters had gone, my husband remarked that it was nearly milking time and that he would start to drive up the cows as his helper had gone hunting. Imagine his surprise, on arriving at the barn, to find the cows already in their stalls. Jack had been there and done his work before going hunting.

---- Mrs. Angela E. Favell, Superior, Wisconsin

Author's Note: This true story is presented here verbatim from the original, and transcribed without editing. It was hand written about 1893 by Angela Haste Favell, my great grandmother. She typed it circa 1920, and lived more than 102 years, passing on in 1953, in Superior. In the later 1800s, about two decades after Thomas Favell, my great grandfather and namesake, returned from four long years in the Civil War, he and Angela homesteaded in a small, quickly built log shelter in forestland east of Upper Lake St. Croix. Later, they cut and hauled logs from that property across the ice to their new land mentioned above. They used those logs to build Shore Acres, their farmhouse around 1890, homesteading and farming this time on the west side of the Lake. Thomas and Angela spoke of Shore Acres as the first house built on the western bank of the lake. We live on the very part of that west side homestead where this story happened about 120 years ago, and sometimes believe we can almost see Jack running to the barn as we look out our south windows here at home. The written word has power and magic to preserve and convey so much over so many years. The many writings of Angela and Thomas remind us of that constancy.

To Check the Trail

Trails and hiking are important in our family's daily lives. As residents of Solon Springs, we have been fortunate that our rural homestead borders a local Douglas County segment of the more than 4,500-mile North Country Trail. Our home and barn are on a high bank overlooking Upper St. Croix Lake and Crownhart Island, which we view many times every day, every year. This is truly paradise.

In winter, as ice cover on the Lake permits, we hike, skate, or ski around the Island nearly every early morning before we head off to work. We and our dogs love the freedom to roam on the ice in those starlit hours, and know it is our shared, silent time each day to give thanks for this source of life, beauty, and peaceful inspiration.

We hike a lot, winter and summer. And some of our best friends once lived just down the timeworn trails from our quiet, old growth forest haven. We will always remember them, our good neighbors, Leon and Edwina, not their real names, but close enough. They had built their own new home about two blocks south of our land, and were enjoying their retirement years there. As Debbi and I got to know them, Leon and Edwina proved to be among the finest people who ever befriended us. They always had time to welcome us to their under-construction home, to feed us, and to chat about the many questions, problems, and fears in life we had as a soon-to-be-married couple.

Leon and Edwina, then both in their seventies, were hard workers, and led aggressively active lives every day. They grew a huge, lush garden, the likes of which we had not seen. Leon was able to coax, into full production, celery, melons, and other sensitive crops, which at that time in the early 1970s, did not grow well in the northwest corner of

Wisconsin. Edwina baked bread, cookies, and other goodies, making their home so cozy.

Any chance we got to visit our Solon neighbors, we did. And we always came away well fed, and well advised about so many things we needed to know. Leon and Edwina were there at just at the right time, when we, as young adults, needed some fill-in grandparents. They served the role for us well, and we were grateful.

Leon often told of their vacation trips to Hawaii, and how Edwina loved sitting in the sun, while he surfed, well into his retirement years. He would animatedly doff his worn railroad cap, and show us the several skin cancer spots on his balding head. "You just gotta keep these covered," he would say, while telling of his adventures on the beaches and riding the waves.

Debbi and I made mental notes every time we got together with Leon and Edwina. These were folks we wanted to be like. They were the finest, nicest people, and so active and engaged with this world and their varied lives. Unfortunately, our own careers soon took us to other parts of the country, and we lost touch with them for several years. Though we wrote back and forth, we did not get to see either of them before their passing on.

At one point, Edwina had told us in a letter how Leon took a late afternoon hike nearly every day, returning to their home by way of the well-worn forest trails connecting our properties. Several large Norway pine trees towered in a clearing on the south side of our land, and she wrote of how she would check down the trail there at suppertime to find Leon on the last part of his route home. He would often sit on the soft, mossy ground, leaning his back up against one of the giant pines so he could nap in the sun. She'd wake him, and they would walk home hand in hand for supper.

One day, she said, he had not returned for supper on time. So as usual, she went to check the trail, and to look for him. Up ahead, she saw Leon, asleep in the sunlight against one of the big pines. She walked up and tried to wake him, but could not.

Leon had fallen asleep for eternity in that serene, sacred place. He had left her on that brilliant day to go on ahead to check the trail and surf the stars. We knew that Edwina, in all her sadness, was glad for him, and for how he could spend his last moments in the forest he loved so deeply.

We walk those same trails nearly every day now, and we revere Leon's tree each time we pass it. Our active dogs need much exercise, so as we leave for a hike, we always say to them, "Let's check the trail!" Checking the trail has become their daily job and our joy.

Someday, a long time from now, I trust, when the sun is shining in the giant pines, and it seems a good day to hike away, I will think of Leon and Edwina, our good friends and many-faceted mentors. And if you are looking for me that day when I don't come home for supper, be sure to check the trail.

Adam's Elephant

An elephant resides in our safe deposit box. Really, sort of...

When our older son, Adam, was about four years old, he accompanied us to our nearby small-town credit union in northern Wisconsin. We set up a new safe deposit box there to store some important things. House documents, birth certificates, precious family pictures, and other items are so important to keep safe. At home, we carefully selected the paper documents and other items to put into the small box we could afford. Adam watched us prepare these.

When we got to the credit union vault, we opened our box and carefully put in the things we brought from home. We carefully noted each important item we stored. As we finished, Adam took a small, shiny-gold ceramic elephant out of his pocket. As I recall, Santa had brought it to him.

Adam said, "Put this in, too." We did.

The years passed rapidly, and so many family and life changes happened. Our parents and one sister passed on, we moved many times, and the family farm was sold. Birth certificates, insurance papers, old driver's licenses, and now death certificates, plus the myriad other evidence we have been alive and active in a document-directed society, have accumulated in our safe deposit box. Someday, we will go through it all, and sort things we no longer need.

Through all of these changes, the silent watcher has been Adam's elephant. He has seen the ins and outs of all our items. In that safe, secure, out-of-sight-and-mind place, Adam's elephant has been guardian of our important things, a role to which Adam wisely appointed him so many years ago.

Adam's elephant has watched the changes of our lives. Yet, with all our comings and goings to get to this point in life, the elephant has been an oft-forgotten but so-important constant for us. He is always there, as are our memories of Adam when he was little.

Adam has moved on now to career and marriage, with his own home and items to secure. We think of him often in his distant, hurried, responsible life. Though we keep in touch as best we can, we wonder and marvel at his new demanding world, knowing we can never fully enter again.

Next time we go to our safe deposit box, I think we will get Adam's elephant and send it to him. I bet he could use his faithful guardian to watch over him and his own important things.

For us, Adam's elephant has been a silent reminder of continuing trust and love from such an innocent time. The elephant has been a good companion in our trip through the formal things of life.

Adam needs him now.

Skateboarding to Retirement

On July 1, 2005, I retired from my clinical career, as well as from my fulfilling life as a university professor. What an honor to receive the title *professor emeritus*. After a several-decade gap, I again took up full time my lifelong interests as writer and creator of new ideas in words and music, with strong hopes to invest all the rest of my renewed life and career here, at our unique northern land of the Red Pump. The warmth of liberation and realization of release were incomparable. This began my re-*tire*-ment, only in the sense of figuratively getting new tires, and then heading fast and far in some new exciting directions yet to explore.

A few weeks prior to that official separation date, I skateboarded to my retirement luncheon. Yes, I rode my skateboard from my university office a half-mile or so over to where the lunch gathering was taking place, popped the board up in my arm for carrying, and propped it against the wall of our meeting room as I walked in. It was a most memorable beginning to a memorable milestone of transition for me.

So, why skateboard to retirement? Two reasons: It was a clear, bright day that just spoke of needing to get out on the downhill long board. And, I wanted to forevermore say that I rode my skateboard to my University of Wisconsin - Eau Claire retirement lunch celebration. Guess I was making a statement.

But what was that statement? Two main points: 1. Thank the Lord, and my always-health-conscious family, and all powers that be, that I am healthy and fit as I retire. I know so well that things could be vastly different. 2. Skateboarding is a fun celebration of life. Sometimes you just have to do the things that bring you joy, and remind you what really is important to you.

OK, maybe there was some ego involved there, too. It does feel good when someone says, "Hey look at the old guy on the skateboard. Jeeezz, he's pretty good." Yes, I have to admit I am not immune to that type of encouragement.

But there were other reasons I now understand better. So many aspects of life were becoming clearer to me in that, my first year of retirement. Let me explain.

I learned to skateboard when I was about ten years old, around 1960. Soon after that, the song by Jan and Dean (I'm sure you know it.), "Sidewalk Surfin'" came out. It was so popular, and strongly influenced my and many others' interest in flying downhill at great speeds on our own feet, always under complete control, of course… more or less.

As a life-long skier, my Dad and ski mentor, Victor, who successfully grappled gravity for all of his nearly 91 years of life, enthusiastically encouraged me to skateboard. He saw it as awesome off-season ski training and fantastic fun. By an early age, I was already skilled at gliding through slalom and downhill ski race courses in the winter while standing on "boards", so the overwhelming appeal of going fast on my feet under the free pull of gravity, AND DURING THE SUMMER, was just too seductive. A world of new fun and challenge had opened to me.

This skateboarding stuff was my dream come true: to be able to soar down the sidewalks and streets, my spring-summer-autumn ski slopes, and turn, jump, tuck, stop, and even wipe out sometimes, so much like on skis. Wow. The sidewalk surfer, the skateboard, was my ticket to a sort-of-year-around skiing.

The years passed. Life, careers, and family happened. My wife, Debbi, and sons, Seth and Adam, gave me my brand new Sector 9 Longboard for Christmas in 1998. I was hooked again. They soon got their own Sector 9 skateboards, too.

Then, in the summer of 2002, Debbi and I saw Jan and Dean perform at the Northern Wisconsin State Fair in Chippewa Falls. My whole appreciation for them, their skateboarding song, and for sidewalk surfing changed forever.

As you may recall, Jan Berry co-wrote "Sidewalk Surfin'" with his collaborator, Dean Torrence, both from southern California. Both also, I maintain, were largely responsible for the still-developing skateboarding craze (and eventually, I submit, for snowboarding, too). You may remember another of their stories-in-song, "Dead Man's Curve" about a serious car accident while guys were racing their cars on the back roads. Something similar happened to Jan in 1966; a true gravity storm, as 'boarders might say. He survived the near fatal crash, but with severe brain injuries and multiple disabilities.

When we saw Jan and Dean in concert that night in 2002, Jan performed with the group, but sat on a chair while on stage. He used a cane to walk, and tried his best to sing. The other group members, especially Dean, his old friend and music-business partner, helped him out. They put on a thrilling show.

My take-home message? These guys were still playing, still performing, and were still the original promoters of the fun-for-life sidewalk surfing hobby that many of us will always enjoy. And they were keeping on with their music in the face of incredible adversity! Jan passed away in 2004, but he had inspired us once again that night at the fair.

That could be enough of a message in itself. But the one I personally took a bit further and thought of as I skateboarded to retirement in July 2005 was: "Thanks for the fun Jan and Dean—and Dad. This ride is for you. I celebrate your lives, and this time of change and reinvention in mine."

So, who knows where the slopes and turns of life will speed us still-striving retirees now? We're just trying our best to avoid those wipeouts and gravity storms from here on. Grab your board!

Hankadookadee and the Worm Bus

Ahhh, the imagination of a four year old.

When our younger son, Seth, was a little guy, we often went fishing on Upper St. Croix Lake and River, near our family's pioneer homestead at Solon Springs, in rural Douglas County. Part of the big adventure of fishing with hook and line with a kid that age is first digging the worms.

We generally headed out, with empty cottage cheese carton in hand, to our moist red-clay and black-dirt garden in Superior. We had mulched in lots of plant material, especially on one end of the garden, and started by carefully turning over the rich soil with Seth's small spade.

Sure enough, there were always lots of worms. Within five or ten minutes of worm picking, we typically had enough worms to last us all morning; at least until an active four year old lost interest, or he and dad got too hungry to fish any more.

One morning, when Seth and I went out to dig worms, we started poking around, and found an especially fat, juicy worm. I figured it would be great for a big blue gill or a crappie.

"No, that's Hankadookadee!" Seth quickly stated.

"Who's Hankadookadee?" I asked.

"He's my sssriend." Seth affirmed, in his four-year old speech.

"Well, I bet he'll catch us a big one." I said.

"No, he's my sssriend!" Seth restated.

"All right," I returned, "Let's put him over here on the other side of the garden so he'll be real happy in the dirt, and let's look for some more."

"OK," he said.

We dug more, and soon found other large worms. It looked like we'd have fish for lunch that day for sure. I could almost smell them frying in cornmeal and vegetable oil.

"NO!" Seth shouted, "Those are Hankadookadee's sssriends and relatives!"

"You mean we can't use these worms either?" the frustrated father said.

"No, these are all Hankadookadee's sssriends." Seth insisted.

"Let's just dig over on that other side of the garden then," I said. "Do you think he knows any of these worms over here?"

Seth thought that would be OK. We soon filled our worm carton and went fishing.

Later that morning, we ran out of worms. As resourceful guys, Seth and I went over to a moist patch of forest dirt and leaves near our tool shed. We poked around with sticks for more worms, and found many just under the damp leaves. I started to put them in our container.

"No!" said Seth. "Those are Hankadookadee's sssriends!"

"I thought his friends were back home in the our garden in Superior," I said. "How did they get here?"

"They took the Worm Bus!" he replied instantly, with an air of "Isn't that totally obvious to everyone?"

For the next year or so, whenever we dug worms, especially near the Red Pump, we had to carefully distinguish which one might be Hankadookadee, and which ones were his friends and relatives. Some were, some weren't. This was important stuff. We always had to be certain before any worm got taken in our worm bucket.

Over the years, the concept expanded. We all began to use "The Worm Bus" as the convenient and obvious family explanation for why and how things, people, animals, events, and anything else in existence could show up instantly and unexpectedly at any place on the planet at any time. No wonder that Seth is now a Ph.D. university professor and research physicist.

The Worm Bus really was and still is a handy explanation for how things can get around without a whole lot of time and effort. Maybe it's for real...

Both our grown, professional sons now live many miles and long hours away. We visit them for holidays and for brief vacations, as possible. The loyal, loving, and rapidly aging father and mother return battered from our fun but grueling road trips to see them; always, it seems to us, through too much ugly urban congestion and road construction.

But we have hit on the solution. No need to ever again drive or fly to visit our cherished boys. From now on--you guessed it--we'll take the Worm Bus.

Puppy Days Are Here Again

Interesting friends help mark the events of our lifetimes. Often, these friends include personable, quirky pets we have loved. All of our family dogs have romped here, near the Red Pump, in all seasons, and eagerly lapped up the clear, cold water from its deep well.

Peppi could climb up and leap over anything, it seemed. A black-and-white Border collie, he had more energy than anyone in the family. He especially liked to fetch things, and to carry around favorite items that belonged to his people. Peppi came to us in 1958, and on the day we met him, he was herding sheep. We watched in fascination as this three-month-old and his parents so intelligently moved sheep around their owners' farm. The owners had named him King, but we knew that wouldn't do if we took him home because it was our last name. We came up with Peppi Puppy, because he had so much energy. That eventually shortened to simply Peppi. Peppi energized our lives until the middle of my university years, when he left us for larger pastures.

The next dog in our lives was Punkin, a Sheltie-mix pup my wife and I rescued from the local pound. We had been married about a year when we met this appealing little mutt in 1976. Punkin had just one eye because of a birth injury, and was a true pumpkin-colored fuzz ball. We easily enfolded her into our home and lives. We hiked often in the forests surrounding the Red Pump. She quickly learned so many tricks: jumping, rolling, sitting, and escaping from just about any enclosure.

For our second Christmas together, the first year with Punkin in the house, we baked our own salt-ceramic tree ornaments to save money. On one of the nights just before Christmas, while we slept, Punkin made the rounds, having escaped her sleeping box, and ate nearly all of the ornaments off the lower levels of the tree. The next morning, we saw (and smelled throughout the house) the scattered evidence of her nocturnal scavengings. Our furious cleaning efforts offset anything we may have saved on ornaments, but we had a great story to tell. Punkin lived with us for another four years or so, until our boys were toddlers and we became concerned about her nipping our little guys. Although we found a nice family for her, we always regretted giving her up. We have missed and wondered about Punkin all the many years since.

Next came Snowball and Tishka, the strapping Samoyed pups who powered into our lives for a short while in the early 1980s. They grew so large so fast, and had such exercise demands. With our own growing children in a busy house, we again realized we had to find what we hoped were good homes for these dogs. Tishka went to a farm family. Snowball went to my parents, both in their late seventies at the time. She became an excellent puller and skijoring dog for my Dad, and a docile, adoring, though very large, lap dog for my Mom. They loved her for her remaining dozen years, and cherished all their Snowball memories.

When our boys were in middle school, we decided as a family that we again needed a dog. She came to us after we went to "just look at the puppies" at a nearby farm. Shiku Ukiuk, an American Eskimo Dog, was our petite, snowy beauty; she joined the family, her pack, when she was eight weeks old. We got her during the particularly rainy, ice-covered winter of 1992. Our studious, language-loving family looked up some appropriate puppy-name possibilities in an Inuit-to-English dictionary we got at the library. The words *shiku* and *ukiuk*, we discovered, could mean *icy winter*. We decided that would be the perfect name for our new pure-white, fluffy family friend. Shiku Ukiuk (aka Shiku, Ukes, Uki, Ukadoo, and so on…) became one of our gang, and, at last count, we had over 40 nicknames for her, some not repeatable here. She was our boys' growing-up dog, and will live on in family stories and legends always. She was a true cream puff with us, a gentle soul at home, who eagerly found and ate blackberries and raspberries right off the bushes on our hikes and runs, and always lifted her leg to pee. Unfortunately, she was also one of the nastiest animals toward others we have ever known. We shared nearly 14 years of fun, travel, and adventures with Shiku, our really good friend through growing years.

Our boys are grown now, pursuing their own lives. Debbi and I live permanently at Kingswood, in our small home near the Red Pump, here in Solon Springs. Our newest family members are Scotty Boots and Molly Mitts. They are brother and sister Sheltie-Border-collie-mix pups who joined our household in fall, 2005. They are small and smart, and they mesh well with our empty-nester lives. Perhaps it is they; perhaps it is we, now as better, more experienced puppy and human parents. We don't know, but we are determined to teach them all the desirable things, and, hopefully, prevent all the bad habits and mistakes that we so wished we had done with our previous canine family members. Maybe we will do it the best yet this time.

It is January 28, 2006 today. Scotty & Molly have been with us now for nearly five months, and fit in fine. We are amazed at how fast they catch on. Puppy days are here again! And now you must excuse me: my underwear have once again left the laundry basket and are making their way up the living room stairs with puppy helpers.

For Molly

Tuesday, February 21, 2006:   The unthinkable has happened. Molly was killed this morning by a passing car on our side road at 5:25 am. Debbi had taken her out, and Molly unexpectedly slipped past all our safeguards, darting off to explore a sound. Molly was hit by the car and killed instantly. The driver, an acquaintance of ours, was kind, stopping immediately to express his apologies and remorse to Debbi. Still in just her robe, pajamas, and slippers in below zero weather, Debbi ran screaming into the house, carrying our little pup, "Molly has been killed. Ohhhhh!"

We placed Molly so gently, so reverently on our inside front-door mat. We hugged and held her close, entwining our hands and fingers in her Sheltie-soft brown, white, and black coat and immersing our faces in her cool, thick, deep fur that still smelled of snowy early-morning forest beauty…and blood. Time stopped. She stiffened, and we allowed Scotty to sniff and be with her.

We took our morning walk with Scotty out on the lake just to free our minds for what was next, and then returned home, our sadness overflowing. We packed up the car at about 8 am, Debbi called in for late arrival that morning at her office, and we drove Molly Mitts, our chubby, chunky, cantankerous chow hound puppy, Molly Collie, to our veterinarian in Iron River, for cremation. We hugged Molly so tightly one last time and said goodbye. Now we are three.

Wednesday, February 22, 2006, the next day: We took our early morning hike in new snow again today, to preserve our routine. Today is our first full day without Molly. It is just the three of us now: Scotty,

Debbi, and Tom. As we came back to our house from our hike on the lake, we noticed that paralleling our footprints to the lake, and just behind us as if trying to catch up, were another set of fresh, small puppy-looking paw prints in the new snow, with no other human prints around. Surely it must be a fox or a cat or a stray puppy alone, or... Our hearts leap! Oh, that it could ever be…?

We have not seen those prints again.

Do Over

When we were kids playing backyard baseball or football, the ball would sometimes get stuck in a drainpipe, hit a house, or bounce under a car moving down the street. Sometimes our pucks would disappear in a snow bank at the neighborhood hockey rink. "Do over!" we'd shout.

As our own boys grew up, they yelled "Do over" a lot when they were playing outside, and especially on their video games. There's even a "do over" reset button on most computer games. It lets you start again, fresh, new, with no mistakes on the record.

My wife and I have always thought it would be great if life came with a do-over rule; when you mess up, you could just yell "Do over!" and automatically get another chance. That has never happened in our lives. Until maybe this past year.

You may recall my earlier essay "Puppy Days are Here Again!" about the great dogs who have shared their lives with us and taught us so much. You may also recall the piece "For Molly" which ends with "We have not seen those prints again." about our sad loss of our new fluffy Sheltie/Border collie puppy, Molly, in a winter accident. Here's what happened after that sad day; a kind of do-over, you could say.

A week or so after Molly was killed, we phoned the family from whom we had gotten her and her brother, Scotty, and explained how she had been hit by a car in the dark early morning of February 22, 2006. We mentioned that, if they ever had puppies again from those same parents, to please let us know; we might seriously consider getting another female puppy from them, because we loved and missed Molly so.

A while later, to our stunned surprise, they called back, saying that indeed their mom and pop dogs were going to have another litter, and we could have first pick of the new pups, all direct siblings to Molly and Scotty.

We drove out to their farm soon after, and eagerly anticipating the bubbling puppy energy of the brown-black-white female replacement for our dear Molly we were about to meet, we ran to their puppy shed. All of the puppies were black and white. Though they all had the same parents, none looked like Molly. We were stunned.

In a few weeks, we came back, looked again, and selected our new black and white "Sonja", more Border collie than Sheltie, to bring home. Our reluctance melted with the spring snow, and we realized that, in a way, we truly were getting a do-over. We were grateful.

As we have watched Sonja grow, now to a remarkably sturdy, strong, substantial, and smart dog with plenty of energy, her idiosyncratic quirks have endeared her to us. She has become Sonja Socks, *aka* The Sock Monster, Sonja Begonia, Ms. Socks, Ms. Begonia, Sonja Bologna and a host of other pet names. She is impressively intelligent, well behaved, and has blended into our home wonderfully well. We are teaching and doing things with her we wish we had done with Molly and all our other dogs. What joy Sonja brings. The Molly sadness is fading.

In all, we wanted Molly back. We were looking for that ever elusive, perfect do over. It didn't happen. We didn't get the full do over we thought we wanted.

But we have learned a lot, and believe we have gained something even more important: We have gotten a chance now for a *Do Better*!

Best of Show

The huge toad almost got splattered by my lawn mower.

I was cutting thick grass and ground cover, near our Red Pump in Solon Springs in June 1985, when my rotary power mower passed over a lump on the ground. The lump looked like a dark rock in the grass, but the rock had bumps and spots on it--and it got up and hopped out of the way as the mower passed. It was a particularly, shall we say, *muscular* toad. I called the boys over.

Seth, age four, and Adam, almost six, playing in another part of our camping area, were thrilled to see the big toad up close. They soon decided he was "Tubby Toad" (he truly was a *tubby* toad), and Seth put him in a box on damp grass and fresh green leaves. The boys decided to take him home to Superior as a pet.

Over the next few weeks with us, Tubby became a fine family pet. Our young sons learned a lot from him, and he was surprisingly interactive with them. They would stroke him gently on the back of his head with their small fingers, and Tubby would warble, his brown and white spotted throat flap moving in and out. They fed him worms and bugs in his box, and always kept a shallow pan of water there for him. Seth took him out many times a day to romp in the damp, dense plants near our Superior garden. He also let Tubby have time to just sit in the low, buggy greenery along one cool side of our house. Toad and boy bonded.

Soon we learned the upcoming summer celebration at the county historical museum included a pet show and contest sponsored by the humane society. Divisions for pets ranged from largest, smallest, and best trained, to best of show across all categories. We saw possibilities for Tubby. Seth asked if he could take his new toad friend to the show.

Debbi suggested that, as a pet show contestant, Tubby should have a proper pet harness and leash. Using some thin gold curling ribbon she had taken from a package, we designed and crafted a small, loose-fitting harness for Tubby. It fit well and was quite attractive for the dark brown toad. "Accessorizing your amphibian," we mused, "what a concept." We also fastened a ribbon lead to the harness so Seth could walk his pet. Wow, a chunky, tubby toad on a gold leash with a tow-headed, blue-eyed four-year-old kid walking him: a winning combination, we figured.

On the day of the contest, Seth put Tubby's harness on the cooperative toad, packed him in his homemade port-a-toad box, and took along his leash. Seth and all of us were excited as we drove to the historical society museum to show Tubby. Each child with a pet had a chance to come up in front of the group as everyone met out on the bay-front lawn of the museum. It was a sunny, brilliant blue day there, overlooking Lake Superior. The kids all sparkled as they each enthusiastically told about their animals and showed them to the crowd of assembled pet lovers.

When it was Seth's turn, he walked to the head of the group, carefully holding Tubby, then put him down on the ground with both his harness and his gold leash attached. Seth told his pet's name, and explained how he got him. Tubby apparently understood his role at that point (or was scared stiff), for as if on cue, he hopped out ahead on the grass while Seth walked him back and forth a few steps in front of the judges and crowd. The audience laughter and approval were huge. Tubby, nonplussed, almost seemed to enjoy it.

The judging of dogs, cats, rabbits, ferrets, turtles, frogs, and other critters was soon completed, and the prize announcements came for each category. Tubby won the first place blue ribbon for the "Interesting Pet" category. When all the division awards had been announced, the drama built as the "Best of Show" trophy was about to be awarded. The head judge got everyone's attention, and intoned loudly "The Best of Show award goes to.... Tubby Toad and Seth King!"

We cheered and laughed; we *knew* Tubby was a winner. Tubby and Seth won a surprisingly large trophy, and we recall the story being in the local paper. We also got some great pictures we will always treasure. Seth had the trophy in his bedroom for all his growing up years. It is stored on a special, revered shelf in our barn attic here at Solon Springs to this day.

After the pet show, we decided to return Tubby to the wild. Putting him back in the lush leaves near the Red Pump was our first thought. We realized, however, that might be too risky for him, with all the wild predators here, and the power mower cruising over his head several times each summer in our camping area. We concluded the protected, moist perennial covered area near our garden at home in Superior might be best for him until hibernation time came in the fall. The spot we decided on was fenced in, and seemed to provide enough freedom for Tubby to hop, eat, and roam. It also offered protection from birds, cats, and traffic, as well as from other kids and parents. We felt Tubby would be secure and happy there for a few more months until the weather cooled off.

Then fate stepped in. In late summer of 1985, we found we had to sell our Superior home and make a major family move south, to another Wisconsin town, because of care issues for our extended families. We packed and prepared for several months, and got entangled in all the depressing details and stresses of moving. It was sad and difficult for all of us to leave our simple, small (but to us, most beautiful) home we had built on our own, on our little corner lot, and had loved for more than a decade. It was also when Debbi and I stopped sleeping well in our lives. We began pulling a much bigger family-care and financial load.

In all the rush and changes, we largely forgot about Tubby. We looked for him once or twice in the garden area where we had last seen him, but could not find our toad. Seth was concerned about this, but he and Adam both understood Tubby needed to be in the wild. Hopefully that was where he was. Just maybe, he had escaped our garden to better digs, literally perhaps, in the larger yard or in our neighborhood.

We resolutely stopped looking, and continued about our intense business of packing and transporting all the important things, indoors and out, we had accumulated in our wonderful, eleven active years in Superior. Debbi hastily dug out some of her treasured flower bulbs and other perennials, and we boxed and carted them to our new home in southern Wisconsin. It truly broke our hearts to leave our well kept, self-built home and yard, with so many memories and so much life having happened there. But we knew we had to leave for a greater family purpose.

One day in late fall of 1985, we were in our new yard transplanting some of those bulbs and plants from the few boxes we had quickly stuffed in Superior as we packed to go. As we carefully tipped out the roots with rich black dirt from back home to replant them, one of the lumps we found in the dark soil moved. *Tubby?* Yes, it appeared to be Tubby, a miraculous reminder of home, our *real* home, not this strange, new one. We thought at first it was too good to be true; that our stowaway friend was just another toad who had bedded down for the fall in our moist northern garden. But the closer we looked at him, and as we watched him move and interact with us, Seth and all of us knew it was our favorite amphibian. We believed it really was Tubby Toad, concluding he had moved with us. We collectively, carefully placed him in our new side garden of dense plants and bushes, to continue life with us at our new home. Tubby was there in those bushes the next spring of 1986, and we kept track of him well into that summer when we last saw him.

Tubby Toad was a good pet for us. He was a needed, fun friend for a four year old and his family at a time of such sad leavings and new, uncertain beginnings. We learned from Tubby how even the humble and mundane, with imagination and love, can indeed become *Best of Show.* We think of Tubby now and his many, many toad progeny here, especially every time we mow near the Red Pump and see a lumpy dark form in the moist leaves. We need to be careful.

Hey, something just hopped over there. *I wonder...?*

Voyageur Victor

Have you ever seen your 60-something backpacking father vault over a wilderness stream on a bent tree? Neither had I.

My dad, Victor, and I started hiking, devotedly, on Isle Royale National Park in 1968, when I was 18. We began as bumbling backpacking rubes and newbies, but went on to become pretty good at it, making more than 30 Lake Superior crossings and trips to "The Isle" over the years. We traveled via all ways and routes to the Island, by air and by water; we hiked every one of its trails, many times, up and down, back and forth, on every part of the Island. Our estimate was at least five hundred miles total, maybe twice that, as we often hoofed it up and down the backbone of the Island on the Green Stone Ridge and Minong Ridge Trails, plus their other loops and subsidiaries.

For those years, we felt our VK & TK hiking duo owned Isle Royale. And for many of those father and son bonding years, we lived in binary states of either (1) being on the Isle, or (2) strategizing about how soon and how long we could get to and be on the Isle. Isle Royale consumed us. It was and is one of the remaining coolest and hottest destinations on earth, literally and figuratively.

Our five acres at Solon Springs, which eventually became home to the Red Pump and our water well, played an important role in our backpacking junkets to Isle Royale. Voyageur Victor, his trekking genes and instincts alert from his generations of durable northern Canadian Metis and strong German heritages, was right at home in our northern Lake Superior paradise of wild forests, streams, swamps, bogs, and inland lakes. He taught me a lot.

We would drive from our family's home at that time in the more settled west central part of Wisconsin ("The *start* of the north," he'd say), to the relatively wilder Solon Springs area ("The *heart* of the north," per Voyageur Vic). We camped there often, and Vic named it "Kingswood" in 1968. It became our staging point for our always next-day, very-early-morning drive to Grand Marais, Minnesota, where we'd board either the Wenonah or Voyageur I (then II) boats to Isle Royale.

Although this whole process began in days prior to our well and the Red Pump, as we would come to know it, we camped in the forest glen very near to where these would eventually be placed in 1973. Indeed, we typically returned to Kingswood from our Isle Royale trips so thirsty and dehydrated that we often said, in those pre-pump days, we needed a better well and water source here. The rigors of our arduous but completely relaxing and fun Isle Royale escapes were ultimately important catalysts in causing us to make the well and pump happen.

But back to our first trip together. We were headed to this Island haven, which Victor had heard about and dreamed of since he was a child. It was to be just a quick up and back trek this time, to check out the Isle, in hopes of doing more hiking and camping on it soon. We overnighted at Solon Springs, and before daylight the next morning, we headed up Highway 61, the scenic north coast road of Minnesota. We completed the four-hour drive, marveled at some of the best scenic territory in the world, and arrived at Grand Portage in time to get our car parked and set for several days. We hoisted our packs and hiked down to the Wenonah boat dock for our nine am departure on this inaugural Isle Royale adventure for us. The boat was waiting, and we were soon, excitedly, finally, on the Wenonah.

Our captain and boat pilot on that day (and many future others) was Stanley Sivertson, long-time Isle Royale resident, Lake Superior and Isle Royale history repository, and our legendary guide about whom we had read. We listened and learned as Stan took us near the ancient cedar "Witch Tree" growing from a stark north coast cliff of dark basalt. We also cruised near the Rock of Ages Lighthouse as we neared the Isle, and saw many other landmarks Stan knew and described; all catalysts for his engaging stories of Lake Superior and Isle adventures from other days. Stan explained and relived so much for us that day, making Isle Royale and the north coast come alive on our first trip over to his ancestral adventure land. We realized our own Island adventures were just beginning, knowing they would be many and memorable, over numerous years to come.

Victor and I were already experienced campers and canoe trippers, having done many miles and portages in northern Ontario and Wisconsin for years, but had never backpacked, being completely self-contained on foot, for more than a few miles at one time. This was our shake-down cruise on foot, to see what lay on the island, to see how we would hold up under load for many miles and days, and mainly to experience first hand what we needed to know and do more of in order to become better backpackers. We hoped to make a base camp at the Windigo campground on Washington Creek, and plot day-hikes or longer routes from there. That had been our simple, original plan.

Our lessons began. The campground had a few small, screened-in Adirondack-type shelters, all of which were occupied by other campers when we hiked into camp. Most of the prepared ground tent sites were also full on that hot, early-August day. It was all more crowded, congested, and noisier than we had anticipated. Park rules at that time allowed backcountry wilderness camping, away from other established campgrounds, so we kept our packs on our backs, smiles on our faces, and trekked farther out on the Huginnin Cove Trail. We hoped to hike the five miles there by late afternoon, and make our own low-impact camp in the forest, or near the cooler, rocky Lake Superior coast on the north side of the island.

As newbies, we didn't make it. We hiked about three difficult miles, then decided we were tired and overheated first-timers, who had endured a long, demanding day of car, boat, and foot travel...and travail. Making camp in a small clearing just off the trail seemed a good idea. It is amazing how naive and ignorant we were then. At that time, we cooked using only small, discreet wood fires; we had no camp stoves. Camp stoves would develop later in availability and affordability, and eventually became integral parts of our repertoire of backcountry technology and skills. Fortunately, we were skilled at making, starting, and maintaining our compact, safe, effective wood campfires, and then extinguishing and obliterating most signs of them. The weather was dangerously hot and dry, so fire starting was way too easy.

On this first trip, we had also not yet learned of the critical need to boil all drinking water on the island for at least five minutes. We just didn't know, and drank water dipped directly from streams and from Lake Superior. It seemed clear and pure, and we believed we were fine doing it. That was how we drank in northern Canada on our canoe trips at that time. Further, our tent was, by today's standards, large and cumbersome, though for the time, it was what we called "state of the Kmart art" for low-budget campers. The box said it was a "pack tent", but we found it was more for packing in our car than on our backs for long distances. Again, we were learning. We gained a lot of knowledge and experience each day and with each step, and made many mental notes of what to do better on our next Isle trip.

We debated heading down the Feldtmann Lake loop, on to the bog trails and board walks, or up the Greenstone Ridge Trail to the Ishpeming Fire Tower, or over to the Minong Ridge Trail we had heard was rugged and undeveloped at that time – all great routes that later became so familiar to us. But as first-timers, we decided to try the easier route, and maybe one that was cooler and wetter on those hot August days. The next day we hiked in to Huginnin Cove, enjoying the Lake Superior breezes, Ontario views, and frigid, deep waters. We waded and swam, and were almost unbearably hot and thirsty. So…we combined powdered vanilla pudding mix with an envelope of hot chocolate mix in our plastic shaker jug, filled it with cold Lake Superior water dipped far off shore from our rock perch, and shook it all up, vigorously.

Incredibly good. We savored our impromptu big lake chocolate shake. It almost defied description; so welcomed that day. We enjoyed every drop, and yes, we know we broke all rules of safe water we later learned so well. I don't even want to think about it.

Some other important memories are lasting lessons we continue to learn from all our lives. One which I replay from that first Isle Royale trip is of Dad and I crossing a remote stretch of Washington Creek as we hiked back from Huginnin Cove, on the rugged north Lake Superior coast of the Island. We decided to go overland for part of the way in order to explore more of the true-wilderness back country, and eventually found ourselves far into a muskeg swamp that only got less and less passable as we tried to move toward the Washington Harbor Ranger Station. We found the stream, but could not cross it because it was too deep and fast. We were under full packs that were way too heavy, plus carrying canteens, fishing rods, and other ungainly, superfluous items that made us work too hard and be too unbalanced for above-water acrobatics on logs. We were learning a lot about what not to take backpacking next time. So we kept hiking cross-country in the general direction of Washington Harbor, but never could get across the stream that blocked our way directly back to the main trails. We were clumsy, dehydrated, and tired now, with our big loads, and could not safely ford or walk across the fast, powerful yard-deep water on rocks or downed logs. We kept hoping for that miraculous, soon-to-be-found "easy" place to cross, but the terrain only got more difficult. We were going way out of our way in the swamp now, and the light was waning. We were worried.

Voyageur Victor, then over 60 years old, said, "Follow me. Watch this." With his full pack and gear on his back, my five-foot, six-inch, 165-pound Dad slithered in close to a large cluster of 15-foot tall, 4-inch diameter alders growing on the stream bank. He got a firm grip on one of the trees with both hands, and climbed hand-over-hand up and out on it. He was six feet in the air now. The tree began to bend, leaning over the stream, toward the other bank. He was hanging over the deep, fast water, so close to the other shore, yet still so far away because of the swift current and our heavy packs.

The tree now leaned horizontally over the rushing stream, with my father hanging like flopping new wash on a clothesline, and moving steadily toward the other shore. As he climbed even farther out on the tree, it bent down perfectly from his weight. He dropped adroitly, and dryly, on to the sand of the other bank. It looked as if he had rehearsed this stunt all his life. Maybe he had. I was awed.

"OK, come on over. Just do what I did," he shouted above the stream noise.

As an otherwise know-it-all 18 year old, I imitated his moves, more out of awe and admiration for my supposedly "elderly" dad on this dream trip, than out of any skill or confidence I actually possessed. It worked. I made it across on the first try. The old guy really knew what he was doing. Now on solid ground, we rearranged our flopping gear, checked our topo maps, and hiked the final miles to connect with our return boat. We got back to the mainland and started home, with, of course, an overnight camping stop in red-pump territory at Solon Springs.

Voyageur Victor's impulsive, gutsy problem solving worked. His creative approach to a hard situation impressed me then, and I have remembered, applied, and modified it many times since. Sometimes in life, you've just got to go for it, I learned, even in a dark, mosquito-dense muskeg swamp on Isle Royale when you are lost with your maybe-not-quite-so-old Dad.

Land of Giants

About a ten-minute walk, less than a mile, from our forest homestead and the Red Pump is a magical, unique site for northland adventures and memories. Now known as Lucius Woods, this 40-acre tract of huge pines, streams, bridges, trails, berries, beach, and wildlife has been the setting for innumerable days of northland family fun. A flood of wonderful memories comes to mind as I think of Lucius Woods State Park, now a well-known Douglas County park and campground in Solon Springs, and home to the Lucius Woods Performing Arts Center. Some of the following stories are recounted from century-old photographs and from my discussions with older family members; most however are my own memories from direct personal experiences in the park for nearly six full decades.

My mother's side, the Favell, Olsen, and Gates families, came to Superior and Duluth in the 1880s and 1890s. They recreated at, and eventually owned property or lived in, Solon Springs (called by many the Native name of "White Birch" until about 1896), first visiting here in the mid-late 1880s. Some based here from about 1890 to 1918-1920, and then from 1950 through the present, so we have many shared family stories that include the adventure parkland that is now Lucius Woods. I am the third generation of my family, since the later 1800s, to retire, build, and live on this land in Solon Springs with my own family members in my sixth decade of life.

The stories summarized here are faithful and accurate, although I reserve the right to tweak exact dates as I learn more. This is an attempt to preserve the essence of some of our family's early Lucius Woods memories and a few morsels of park history. In approximate chronological order, here are a few vignettes:

■In 1897, my aunt and uncle, Mabelle and Clough Gates, are pictured biking on what is now Main Street, the northern park border. We also have a circa 1904 picture of them skating on clear, open lake ice near what has become the park's beach and picnic area. In both cases, they are dressed in their long, formal finery from the period. People sure seemed to dress up more then. We have numerous photos of such period activities in many seasons.

■In the summer of 1914, and at other times, my mother, Madeline, then age three, often played and swam at the beach with her dad and mom, my grandparents, Ernest and Inga Favell. The photos of them are curious and interesting, and now seem so quaint, although they were modern folks for their own time. They lodged at my great grandparents Thomas' and Angela's then-new home and popular boarding house, Piney Ridge, on the central east-west street, now Main Street, in Solon Springs. The park still adjoins this street on its northern border.

■The swimming pictures mentioned above show a wood-frame water slide coursing down from the shore of Lucius Woods into the shallow water of the Lake St. Croix beach. It looks like fun. I wonder if it became a toboggan slide in the winter? Wish I could ask.

■My mother, Madeline, danced with local Native people at powwows in a park near what is now Lucius Woods in the summer of 1914, and at other times. We still have her three-year-old, little girl's fringed dancing dresses and moccasins stored at home, plus pictures of some events of those early Solon Springs days with First Nations neighbors.

■In early years, the Waterbury family owned the nearby creek area and forest in what is now the park. Now called Park Creek, the rushing, clear trout stream was then known as Waterbury Creek. One day, around 1910, while he was fishing surreptitiously from the stream bank, my grandfather, Ernest Favell, called "Doc" by many, caught a sizable trout, a German Brown, he told me when I was very young. He was not supposed to be fishing on the Waterbury private property, and hid the quickly-unhooked, wildly-flopping trout in his shirt so he could carry on a friendly chat with Mrs. Waterbury, who had just then come by on her daily stroll down the creek-side trail. So that we would all remember his adventure, Grandpa, a DO general-practice family physician, painted a pastel chalk picture titled "No Fishing" to commemorate his catch. Only our family knew what had really happened that day on the creek years before with the venerable, pesky local doctor and Mrs. Waterbury. His painting still hangs in the Solon Springs Historical Society Museum, and can be viewed by anyone visiting the living room of the old log home there. Ernest John Favell's paintings were numerous and well known. The backstories of his prolific work as "Artist-Doctor of Northern Wisconsin" per his letterhead, are interesting, and must be told in later volumes of these Tales.

■For as long as I can remember, my parents and grandfather referred to the Lucius Woods creek trail, with its towering Norway and White Pines, as *The Land of Giants*. They also said it was a magical place where elves and gnomes likely lived and watched us, as we enjoyed the quiet, ancient beauty of that cool, moist stream valley.

Today, whenever we walk those paths among our giant elders growing there, I still feel the same sense of majesty and reverent awe I did as a young boy on those trails nearly sixty years ago. This precious bit of paradise, I trust, will always be here in Solon Springs at Lucius Woods, where nature and imaginations thrive unbounded by time.

Explorations in the Park

Some places remain special to us all our lives. In the first portion of this four-part series about Lucius Woods Park, I recounted a few of our family's stories from early days in this adventure-filled Land of Giants in Solon Springs, just down our road. The memories I shared were many second-hand ones, conveyed to me from pictures and family tales passed on since the 1880s. This part on explorations is set in the 1950s-1960s, and covers many more of my own boyhood experiences and stories, and thus some more history of the Park. My many first-hand Lucius Woods memories include:

■While walking barefoot on gravel roads in the park in 1954, I felt something on my four-year-old leg. I looked down, and saw a small striped snake wrapped around my ankle. I just pulled it off, no big deal. Guess that's why they are called *garter* snakes.

■In those years, my family often tent-camped in the park. When I was about eight, we had a strong hailstorm one hot July day. As we peered out of our tent after the storm, it seemed as if deep snow had fallen all around, with white, gleaming contoured deposits at least an inch or two thick. The campground-covering hail "smoked" water vapor throughout the park. All of us camp kids rushed out of our tents, reveling in the snow-white ice piles in humid mid July.

■Lucius Woods had a distinct summer smell in those days. The array was a complex combination of wood smoke from campfires, along with odors of the damp, sealed logs of the beach changing house, picnic pavilion, and benches, all made from big local pines. The smells of pine sap from cut branches, smoke, mold, tent mildew, suntan lotion, rubber air mattresses, camp cooking, and, of course, bug repellent all filled the air. Sniffing the summer air there now still recalls those days of family fun fifty-plus years ago.

■It was exciting entering the individual knotty-pine-paneled changing stalls at the sand-beach changing house to hurriedly get ready for swimming adventures. Shouts of kids playing in the water of the sandy beach always made me rush. I couldn't wait, and could never move fast enough to get out and have fun with them. I thought the round door latch sign that rotated to say open/occupied on each personal stall in the changing room was interesting. How many times I forgot my towel, t-shirt, diving mask, or fins in a stall where I changed, and had to come back later in the day to get them. They were always still there. Nothing disappeared. Diving for clams in the beach area was serious work then for a 10-year-old kid.

■The log changing house and restrooms at the beach seemed damp and dark, with many crevices and cracks. Large wolf spiders lurked in the cool corners, and amazed me. They were making a living, in that protected environment, on the smaller critters that happened through their well-cloistered territory. They were so interesting, never scary.

■My dad, Victor, often kept a galvanized milking pail of hot water on our fire when we camped at Lucius Woods in those years. He and my mom, Madeline, cooked peeled ears of sweet corn in it. Salt and butter were kept handy on the picnic table nearby. We ate fresh corn whenever we wanted. We'd pour out some of the hot water for washing dishes or hands throughout the day, adding more water to the bucket from the hand pump located in the middle of the campground. We tended our small fire carefully, keeping it going safely all day and night, especially in wet weather. We could not afford a gas camp stove then.

Lucius Woods is an amazing, unique northland paradise. It remains one of the most magical, wonder-full places in the world, continuing to be a comforting, constant refuge around which so much of our lives revolve. Park adventures carried into our next phases of life, through some tumultuous years.

Growing up with Pines

Life moves on. Mine sure did. Childhood days in Solon Springs, at Grandpa Favell's Cozy Cove lake cabin and at this family forestland, passed into teenage years. I got busy with other important things in life, and Lucius Woods became a less-frequented but no-less-cherished escape. The Vietnam War, Watergate, high school and university years, and a changing world all offered challenges of their own for our nation and our family. The Park was a welcomed refuge for us. Some of my Lucius Woods memories from the 1950, 1960s, and beyond involved my growing social and perceptual senses. Some of these stories include:

■During the summer of 1958, we camped often in the park. One weekend we saw William Proxmire kick off his campaign for full election to the US Senate from Wisconsin. He had replaced disgraced Senator Joseph McCarthy in a special election the year before. Senator Proxmire spoke to the crowd from the top of the hill in what is now the concert area. No PA system was used; he just spoke loudly. We stood down below the hill on the large open lawn and heard him just fine. I was a highly impressed eight-year old. My folks were impressed too, and voted for him for all his years in the US Senate. From that time on, we followed Senator Proxmire's career, especially appreciating his "Golden Fleece" awards for waste in government spending.

■Making pancakes in the huge open fireplaces in the picnic pavilion was work and fun. My dad and mom did most of cooking and preparations for so many prior years; now I did more of it as I grew and progressed in Scouting. At that time, the large log picnic pavilion on the lake bank had glass windows that swung open, ornate chandelier lighting, and large fireplaces for all to use. We especially liked the fireplace at the south end of the building, with inside and outside access to it. You can still see where the outside access was on the south end of the pavilion. Our big camp skillet fit into the open-fire cooking area, and, inside or outside, we could make gigantic, thick pancakes a foot or more in diameter. With real homemade maple syrup and butter, we could feed a group of eager, ravenous campers.

■In the pavilion fireplace, we'd cook up the bacon first, then the eggs, then the pancakes, all in our same pan. The bacon grease kept everything from sticking. The aroma of it all, with wood smoke, was wonderful in that enclosed space. As a boy and teen, and an often-resolute Lucius Woods tent camper with the family, I spent many gloomy, rainy, cold days playing and hanging out within the pleasant refuge of that solid log building. Often, it was just my sister Karen and me, but sometimes other kids and families from camp and village would come in to cook or play. It got loud in there then.

■My parents, sister, and I, sometimes with other camp or village families, spent many of our summer days there playing games, reading, sleeping on the tables, cooking, whittling, and just killing time until a storm stopped, or until we got warmed up from an often cold, damp night in our tents. It was boring and tediously awful then, but I'd relive a day of it in a moment if given the chance. Walking into that log pavilion now brings back so many thoughts of those days and people, and the comfort we all knew there together.

■The swimming area had roped-off beginner and advanced areas then, with a metal-barrel/wood-deck raft anchored out deeper. We swam and dove off that raft all day. A mark of courage among us 7 to 12 year olds was to dive to the bottom, then search for and bring up rocks, without using the diving board. Our days sped by on that raft; up and down, in and out of the water. I was always hungry.

■As an older teen who could drive, in 1966 and 1967, I camped with high school friends at Lucius Woods. Yes, girls were getting to be very important in our lives. Nonetheless, as science fiction fans, all, we geeks thought we could be authors and brought our typewriters. We each determined to use our park retreat to write something significant we could sell to a magazine. None of us did. But we had fun swimming, lazing around camp, and combining random opened cans of food into one-pot meals we heated over our fire, doing as little work as possible. It was a hot, dry, beautiful week, and we mostly just basked in the sun and did little else. When I told a visitor I was the main cook of group, one of my geek friends said "No, not really. You just open the cans." It was true, but we didn't starve.

In the early 1970s, Debbi and I found each other, and were married in 1975. Over the next several years, our other great loves, sons Adam and Seth, followed, and we all shared often in the treasures of Lucius Woods. The next chapter will cover some Lucius Woods memory snapshots of our more recent, young family adventures in that incredible park, our Land of Giants.

Giants through Adult Eyes

Our family's Lucius Woods adventures began in the 1880s-1890s, continuing through today. Previous parts of this Solon Springs series recounted some earlier park memories. To conclude, here are a few of our more recent remembrance snapshots:

■In the early 1970s, my parents Madeline and Victor, and I, as a maturing young adult, along with friends, camped among the pines often. Often, my folks and I conversed deeply and fully in new ways as we walked among the large trees on Park Creek trails during difficult family and national events. The ancient trees, along with peaceful sun-dappled creek waters, comforted us and provided thick-green forest insulation from a world of troubles then in those tumultuous Vietnam War, Watergate, and Nixon impeachment years.

■In the winter of 1976-1977, Debbi and I skied the park trails and snow-covered lake with our small, new puppy, Punkin, an orange/white Sheltie-mix. We carried her in Debbi's warm jacket hood, perhaps a canine precursor to the "snugglie" packs we soon would be using with our own little guys.

■With our infant and toddler Superior sons in the late 1970s and early 1980s, we day-hiked the park trails in summer and fall. Younger son, Seth, at age 2 or so, would stop, try to block our way, and say "Carry me, carry me…" until we did. Older son Adam got us playing "Pooh Sticks" at each bridge, something we still do today. No stick now is safe around us from being dropped from a bridge and floated in a race with other; some days, it's *Extreme Pooh Sticks.*

■In winter, we marveled at the marshmallow world of snow-frosted forest and icy streams around us, and often hiked or skied on the frozen lake. In summer, we'd camp, swim, and hike in the park, as we relaxed on so many hot days and nights in the lush piney coolness surrounding us.

■As a growing young family in the 1980s-1990s, we swam at the beach and dived from the raft with friends. It helped our young boys become strong swimmers. We often canoed to the beach from farther down the lake. The guys learned to paddle well, and experimented with swamping and righting our canoes safely in the shallows near the park beach.

■With all our water fun, swimming, diving, and canoeing, we often got "duck itch" from parasites in the water. We learned to use the hose at the beach house to spray off the mites before they could penetrate to the *really* itchy stage, at least most of the time.

■My folks walked with their grandsons in the park, passing on stories and thoughts of tall trees and trails in this Land of Giants. Each time we visited the park, we eagerly checked on "The Captain", the giant old White Pine near the first bridge. We were saddened when it broke in a storm and died. We walk near it still.

■In 1982, a friend contracted Lyme disease from a tick bite she apparently got in the park woods. This young mom developed severe complications. It was the first we knew much about Lyme disease, and a reminder that bug repellent and tick checks are good ideas much of the year.

■Around 1991, Seth and I missed our Cub Scout pack's official Webelos father-and-son campout, so we had our own at Lucius Woods. We still talk about that special adventure when we hike or bike by "our" campsite in the park. Also, somewhere around that time, we realized the word "camper" had changed. It no longer just meant a person; a camper had also become a thing, a vehicle.

■We often visited the park bateau shelter on the hill to see the traditional bateau (*flat-bottomed boat* in French) housed there. Adam enjoyed it as a big toy and model. Later we heard it got moved to the Fairlawn Museum in Superior due to vandalism.

■Work, family, and distance occupied our time over the next many years. We finally saw our first Lucius Woods Performing Arts Center concert in the late summer of 1997, an excellent Celtic group. Wow. We have been eager concert regulars and volunteers since 2002. This past winter, Debbi and I were especially pleased to compose and author our original song "Makin' Music in the Park!" the new Lucius Woods Performing Arts Center theme song for its 15th anniversary year, 2008. It has been so fun to dance to it now when they play the CD over the powerful sound system, and to watch others swing and sway, as the professionally-recorded rendition of our tune plays for the opening and end of each of the eight summer concerts, a total of 16 times in summer 2008. We feel that our song helps us give back a bit to the Park, and to all who love it, for the inspiration and enjoyment we find there.

■We have been volunteer helpers for the Park segment of the 4,500-plus mile North Country Scenic Trail. We also have taken monthly data on Park Creek as part of the statewide University of Wisconsin Extension Water Action Volunteer stream monitoring research program. It was and is our privilege, indeed our local destiny, to be stewards for this special place. We are honored to work and watch on behalf of the trails, creek, and woods we love.

Our family's Lucius Woods memories have spanned a hundred years and more--and the story goes on. The park is just a short walk from our home near the Red Pump, and is a frequent destination for us at all times of the year. Debbi and I have hiked in the park on thousands of silent, sacred mornings, and will hike there, we trust, for thousands more with our boys and their families. That is our hope. We have daily seen the changing stars, sky, sunrises, clouds, waves, and birds; we have watched the lake ice come and go for many years. We will for many more.

What a place to grow older, starting each of our days with our giant elders, the Norway and White Pines who have already outlived us several times. We are pleased to share a small role in the continuing natural and human history of Lucius Woods, just down the road from this land of the Red Pump.

Lila and Syd...those other relatives

Sometimes there are admirable people you'd like to know better, folks you'd like to sit on a boulder around the Red Pump with and just talk for hours...but you never get the chance. And sometimes, believe it or not, they are "those other relatives" you have never really gotten to know well. The years run by in our busy lives, and we realize our chances may be waning to acknowledge how grand some people are. For me, that's Lila and Syd, not real names, but our very real relatives.

Lila and Syd recently celebrated their 64th wedding anniversary -- along with their 90th and 91st birthdays, all occurring on the same day. What planning. They have been stalwart workers and caregivers throughout their lives, and they deserve all the celebration that can come to them now. I learned only too late how they endured myriad family slights and oversights. They have been so supportive when we have needed them, and I wish we could do more for and with them.

For all of their lives together, Lila and Syd worked hard and managed well on their small farm in rural western Wisconsin. They seldom traveled, but raised productive, intelligent, contributing children, and are strong guides for, and seemingly eternal pillars of, their rural community.

Lila and Syd also endured family tuberculosis back in the 1940s and 50s, days when TB meant lengthy isolation for patients in state-run sanitaria. They were separated from their children and family because of the disease, but Lila and Syd made sure their children and other family would not fall prey to the virulent spread of TB. Their love for each other and for their family was, and is, unbounded. Their unselfish actions showed it.

Interestingly, over all the years I have known Lila and Syd, whom I so admire, I have never been to their farm home, and am not quite sure why. But I have talked with them often at many family gatherings, and enjoyed spending time with them. For me, they have always been our family's other relatives, the ones I wish I could have known better and spent more time with, but could not, due to many complex family issues. Among our eldest family members, I revere them so highly.

We were pleased to wish both Lila and Syd exceptionally happy birthdays this year, and many more anniversaries together for years to come. I have a feeling their spiritual and physical strength, plus their positive, smiling, active engagement with the world, no matter what, will assure that.

As is true with so many of our relatives and friends from other parts of Wisconsin, Lila and Syd have never come here to visit us; they've never seen this ancient northern forest, nor drunk the cold water from the Red Pump. "It's too far," some say, not them. A southern Badger state view we hear often in our northwestern part of the state is that we are *up here*, as many phrase it, implying we are far away from them and the other southern Wisconsin population, media, and cultural centers. What they don't recognize is we are simply *here*. That is, we belong here, and reference the world from here. This is home, where we spend and invest over lives. Ours is a world of deep forests and clear lakes; not fields and farms, not clogged highways and sprawling suburbs.

Many Wisconsin residents also don't understand how, here in northwestern Wisconsin, we draw our linkages, loyalties, and references for identity and purpose, culture and commerce, education and medicine, media and entertainment, travel and sports, and more from our varied, vibrant resources in this *Northland* region. Our communications and culture emanate from our Twin Ports of Superior and Duluth, from northern Minnesota, from Lake Superior coasts and waters, from Thunder Bay, Winnipeg, and all of Canada and Alaska, and of course from the Twin Cities of St. Paul and Minneapolis. In reality, we live quite far *south* from most of those daily influences on our lives. We are actually more down than up from most centers that matter to us.

Quite frankly, many here are not necessarily enamored of the southern Wisconsin meccas of the Dells, Madison, and Milwaukee. For a lot of us in this area, *those* places embody the foreign concepts and locations, and are logistically and culturally so far *down there*, a world away in distance and values from what we hold important in the Northland. We are often glad for our geographic insulation here.

A deeply held view among some Native peoples is that all places on Earth can be the center of the world. This is that Center for those of us who live here, and love being here. As it is often used, we view that phrase "up here" as condescending. It implies that some other downward-referenced location is the real center, and that our diverse, complex northland home is a separation from what should be the norm. We respectfully disagree.

But back to Lila and Syd. Even though it is harder now for them to travel north to us, we hope we will go to see them at their center of the world. And who knows, maybe they and others we love and know will also come here, and get to spend some time and life with us near our patient Red Pump, someday.

For Lila and Syd, we will visit at their peaceful, cherished farm home, hopefully for many years to come. We may at last get to know each other better. Lila and Syd are people to learn so much from.

Maybe there is still time for those other relatives to become our *closer* relatives.

What Party Was That?

"So, what party do you belong to?" I've been asked that, and have never quite known what to say. I am not a card-carrying anything regarding politics. Maybe I'm just part of the pine-forest Red Pump Party?

But nowadays, I have had some time to think on these many-faceted, complex issues as I work outside near the Red Pump, and ponder often about what really matters to me. Here are some of my thoughts these days as a rural-dwelling resident of northwestern Wisconsin thinking about this nation in autumn of 2008:

The Green Party speaks my heart-words about our environment, sharing my deep reverence for our natural world. We live in the forest near the lake. Stewarding our natural world and blending in with it are important in this realm.

I also agree with the Democrats about working for the common good and helping all of us to live better lives through public policy initiatives. Democrats seem to care the most about people, health care, education issues, and many other things important to me.

But I find a lot of value in the Independent Party ideals of making my own decisions and being able to choose among candidates and issues on my own. Being able to independently vote, as we each believe best, not because of a party platform pushed on us by famous politicians, is central to our way of thinking here. Independent, objective thought and action are critical to individual and societal success.

The Libertarian ideals, as I understand them, of "educate don't regulate" and of keeping government out of our personal lives have considerable merit. Government that governs least is indeed best, to paraphrase Jefferson. I'll bet we all have much more 'Libertarian' in us than we may think.

The Republican belief in individual efforts and energies being rewarded with individual gains appeals to me, too. I work hard, always have, and so does all of my family. I believe nothing confers dignity on a person in this culture more than working–working to take care of yourself and your family; to achieve your own dreams; and to make your own way in this complex world.

Unfortunately, there are serious downsides to all formal party ways of thinking. These trouble me.

"Green" in this country is too often represented as synonymous with another five-letter word: *f-l-a-k-e*. I wish that were not the case.

Democrats seem to place too much emphasis on everyone sharing, on giving too much away, with not enough value on the innovative, entrepreneurial spirit of motivated individuals that can change our lives.

Independents can be criticized for not aligning on issues, for potentially creating policy checkerboards in governance at all levels. Non-alignment can be insignificant non-effect.

Libertarianism proposes a society with ideally minimal regulation, where we all act wisely on what we each 'know' to be best, and everything works out well. This seems unfeasible for any human world in which I have lived.

Republicans too often seem to fit the stereotype of born on third base but think they hit a triple; the "I got mine, too bad about yours," winner-take-all mindset is still evident in that party.

So, as you can see, I'm conflicted. I believe these political conceptual frameworks all have merit. But they all also have glaring, disturbing deficiencies. At this point in my life, I find I am simultaneously in agreement with, and revolted by, portions of each.

Next time I'm asked what party I belong to, guess I'll say "Hey, I am a staunchly green *Demo-Indepen-Liber-Republ-crat-dent-tarian-ican.*" That'll settle it all, I'm sure.

By the way, be sure to vote.

On By

We can learn a lot from sled dogs. Our totally *un*official, *un*certified, unregistered, and unruly Red Pump dogs, Scotty and Sonja, are eager, trained Sheltie/Border Collie-mix power pullers…. sort of, maybe. They may not be professional sled dogs, but they do focus on the essentials. They know: *Gee*, go right; *Haw*, turn left; *Hike*, charge ahead fast; *Whoa*, stop; and *On By*, ignore irrelevant distractions. Most of us who are pulling hard in our lives and jobs, regardless of our own pedigrees or lack thereof, are pretty good at the first four of these. Our language has many social metaphors for these concepts, going well beyond the physical actions described.

But that last one, *On By*, is still something we all can learn. Getting our work done with out being diverted is often difficult. Tuning out distractions and disruptions in our lives, day and night, is hard to do, and seems to get harder the older we become. Acting upon *On By*, meaning not worrying, not fixating needlessly on concerns about family, work, politics, and so on, gets harder to do as we add to the worry-weight on our individual sleds of life.

Pulling that heavy load takes its toll on us. Curiously, the growing popularity of expensive, designer stimulant beverages and other pick-me-ups we use seems paralleled by growing attention to the array of relentlessly-advertised sleep aids. Our custom as a society appears, increasingly, to be: animate ourselves with some products during the day; try to calm ourselves (and "quiet our active minds," as the ads say) with other heavily advertised products at night. That good night's sleep still seems ever evasive. The use of uppers during the day and downers at night, unfortunately, has been around a long time. Now our ups and downs seem more and more mediated by mass-marketed products and brand names, be they caffeine sources or prescription sleep medications. We are going both ways at once.

Maybe the sled dogs and their drivers have it right. We all need a firm reminder sometimes to just let certain things go *On By*. When we have done what we can about our concerns at home or work, or with our health, family, or finances, we should keep our focus and keep moving ahead – just like the sled dogs do. We can continue *On By*, and not let those worries, distractions, and disappointments lure us off the trail.

Yes, sled dogs can teach us a lot about doing the best we can in the moment, with what we have, and letting the rest of life work out as we run our course. *On By* may be particularly useful to remember at this point in our lives. Not "Hike it up!" press on, pull harder; not "Whoa!" stop trying or caring; but *On By,* give ourselves permission to keep on going, while we let distractions and memories of imperfections remain in the background of our lives. Sometimes it's good just to pet and comb your dogs while you sit on the deck near the Red Pump, and let the world work itself out around you.

Those sled dogs are awfully smart.

Modern Metis: Man in the Middle

Some stories connected with the Red Pump deal with just the basics of being human. Here is one of those. Many of us have always thought we were "white" guys. But it seems, at one time, we must have looked disturbingly different to others in this part of the country. I never thought about it much until lately.

There were times during my younger life when people in my small town would look at me and size me up as not fitting in. We probably all know the feeling, and there can be various reasons. I could tell it was happening to me, but was never exactly sure what they were judging me on. Growing up in the 1950s-1960s in rural west central Wisconsin, I certainly thought of myself as White…yes, with the capital W. That's what I was told and taught in all those years. That is the box I checked on the forms: White. Nowadays, I have found it is not that simple. *Metis* people often find themselves in the middle of culture, races, and labels, and it looks like I am Metis in ethnicity. Many people are.

The more I learn about this, the more pleased I become. As I immerse in this geography, in this northern forest and lake culture I love and in which I have always felt so at home, the prouder I am to know of my probable, partial Metis (*may TEE*) origins. American Metis, that is.

It is apparent I am one of numerous Metis people in the US, a man in the middle of cultures and ethnicities, who is a small portion Native and many parts varied European in ancestry, not really fitting fully into any one on those categories. That's who I have become. Or more correctly, that is who I now know I am, and have been all along; more hybrid than mutt or mongrel, I prefer to think, though all those terms may apply.

Metis, French for "mixed", is a common term in Canada, although it is seldom used in the US. In my case, it means a blend of French Canadian and First Nations, aboriginal heritages with other European ethnicities intermixed. Metis origins are common for many people in the US, probably more so in northern states near Canada, where the term Metis is also more freely used. European settlers and native peoples extensively intermarried and interbred throughout North America, so the mix is common: Native, aboriginal peoples with European immigrant settlers of all varieties in this new land and hemisphere, to those of Euro heritage.

Some estimates are that at least 70 million North Americans are of mixed Native-Euro heritages, although Metis is not recognized in the US as a separate racial grouping. If other Metis have had experiences similar to mine, they probably were not, and still are not well aware of their mixed background, or that there even is a designated term for them...I mean us. In Canada, *Metis* is one of the specific racial categories to mark in official federal, provincial, and other forms. The Metis option is included along with other categories of Asian, Caucasian, African-Canadian, First Nations, and so on, with Metis considered a distinct racial group for government census and data purposes. Regarding our neighbors to the south incidentally, an equivalent Mexican and southwestern US term for mixed Native and European peoples is *Mestizo.*

Now that I am finding out more about my Metis background, it has helped me understand a lot about myself and my growing up in an area of the US settled in the late 1800s by mostly white, northern Europeans. As an example, the older boys in my small town Scout troop at the local Lutheran church referred to me as "bush n*gg*r", "black Norwegian", and "Pepsi". As an 11 and 12 year old, I simply lived with being called that as part of growing up. I didn't really know what the terms meant, or what they derived from at that time, but figured they were my earned nicknames, given me by the older boys whose acceptance I sought. At the time, I recognized there was nothing I could do about it anyway, with the age, size, and strength differences among us, and the fact that even some of the adult leaders used those terms. I was all of those things, I gathered, and just took it as it came. My skin, eye, and hair color, and my "Indian French" looks were what they saw. I had never noticed or thought about it then, because I didn't know any better, and because I didn't understand my mixed background.

Later on, when I became engaged to marry my wife, my new, supposedly so-Norwegian heritage in-laws and relatives, with at least the most recent four or five generations of their families born in the Midwestern US, commented to my fiancée "But he's not our nationality..." That truly hurt and amazed me then; it still does. It was also inaccurate. These were good, loving people who generally meant well, but they did not at that time understand diversity beyond their narrow experiences. They were saying these things about me: a young man born in Wisconsin, USA; of parents both born and living all their lives in Wisconsin, USA; an Eagle Scout; a National Merit finalist and Honors Program bachelor's degree graduate at the University of Wisconsin –Madison; holder of a new master of science degree and working on a doctorate when we got engaged; and who had generations of family in the US military serving in many wars. And yet I was not *their* nationality, not worthy? It seemed a strange concept to me. Comments were made how they had hoped she'd have married someone of their "own" nationality and religion, with obvious disappointment being the undertone.

I had no idea what they were talking about. Wasn't I their nationality? Especially with my Norwegian great grandfather and great grandmother, Ennar and Christina, on my mother's side, who both came directly from Oslo and immigrated to Duluth, Minnesota in the 1880s? And with my mother, Madeline, who spoke, read, and wrote Norwegian, who taught me Norwegian sports and arts, including ski jumping, cooking, rosemalling, and playing a Norwegian mandolin she learned on from her mother, Inga? I had even been an active Boy Scout at and often attended a local Norwegian-culture church for years… But still, something caused that separation. They were only seeing part of me.

I couldn't figure it out, until I realized later how I appeared compared to their Norwegian-American cohort of that time and place, and learned more about my Native side from Canada. My great grandfather, Antoine, I was told by family elders, came from St. Alphonse, in northern Quebec province. Some said he fathered at least 20 children there with at least five women, many probably aboriginal or Metis, in the early and mid 1800s. One of his sons, Gideon, came to northern Wisconsin around 1880 to work in the logging industry. He married Ella, an Ojibwa-Metis woman from northern Wisconsin, possibly following his father's examples in Quebec, and had four children with her. Ella passed away in early adult life, and he then married my German immigrant grandmother, Magdalena around 1880. So, although my actual percentage Metis or Native is perhaps one eighth (12%) or less, I am verifiably one quarter Norwegian and one quarter German, born in the USA of US born parents. And not their nationality?

Still, some folks believe I look different than the Midwestern US mainstream of appearance; I believe that has made the difference in my treatment. Others were seeing things I don't, and basing their stereotypes upon that. The name-calling and references by others to my perceived nationality or racial differences probably stem from facial appearance and body build. In plain words, I don't look German or Norwegian; I do look French Canadian, or as some have said, Indian French. That's just the way it is. To some, I apparently don't look enough like a Caucasian northern European to be "their" nationality, and certainly know full well this can be true for people of other national and ethnic origins in this and other parts of the country.

So, here I am, an ethnically mixed Metis man in the middle. I'm not sufficiently Native or Indian to be enrolled as a member of any Tribe or Band in the US or Canada. Who even knows what tribe it would be after all these years: Inuit, Cree, Ojibwa, a mix of others? How am I distantly related to the northern Quebec mixed-race peoples of the mid 1800s? I'm not sure. But I am also not quite "white" enough, for some it seems, to fully qualify in that racial category either. Race is sure an arbitrary concept, isn't it? For example, my father, Victor, was dark in skin coloration, and dealt with this all his life in twentieth century American culture. He was stopped several times from reentering the US from trips to Mexico in the 1930s and 1940s, my parents recalled, because border officials thought he may be a native Mexican Indian trying to "sneak" into the US.

Food for thought. I sure wish there was a "Metis" box to check next time I have to fill in a form. And too bad I checked "White" all those years. Why? Because it really isn't true. And further, it ignores my own, and many, many others' mixed racial and cultural heritages. It is as if we don't tangibly exist because we are forced into binary, categorical choices that don't apply.

We don't hear much about Metis people in the US. But here I am, along with many unnoticed others, who haven't had vocabulary to describe ourselves. I am one of millions; a mixed race, part Native, part European ancestry person in the US, always having to declare I'm white, when I am really a Modern American Metis: a man in the middle of cultures, races, and labels.

Madeline's Moccasins

Madeline, my mother, and a Solon Springs child adventurer in the early 1900s, was mentored and encouraged by her mother, Inga, and grandmother, Angela. At age three, in the summer of 1914, strawberry-haired, freckled "Maddy" danced with indigenous, Native friends, likely Ojibwa and Fox Indians, at powwows here in the Solon Springs parks.

Later in her life, she often recalled her experiences with First Nations celebrants during that and other summers of her childhood. Faded, bent family snapshots of her and dancers taken then are stored in our albums here, and we have carefully boxed and protected her worn, little-girl's beaded moccasins and fringed dance dresses from those days. Madeline's moccasins and dance dresses remind us of the opportunities, and perils, of embracing diversity; of taking on different, some said *savage* ways, then and now. Madeline was ahead of her time. We are still realizing how much we learned from her diverse, creative interests.

An aware, alert, and always-durable woman, Madeline was the oldest of three other surviving siblings, all brothers. She was a free-spirited naturalist, tomboy athlete, and lifetime learner, constantly interested in knowing more about nearly everything. From their first date at a high-school party in 1927, she became best friend, wife, business partner, and love forever for my father Victor's 91 years. By my estimation, from knowing her, and from reading through her life items now, Madeline was a true progressive: a person of powerful principles and convictions, unafraid to differ from those around her. She studied and admired works of Emerson and Thoreau, as well as Albert Schweitzer, Marie Curie, Eleanor Roosevelt, and other learned men and women of thought, social action, and science. She taught us, living by their words and examples, even in difficult national and family times. I was born when Madeline was 38, forming my knowledge of her mostly in her mid-life years; times of transition, social isolation, family turmoil, and financial strain from the presence of severe, chronic disability in our family. Those were hard years for her. I knew it then, even as young as I was. She committed deeply to those in her care, and consistently did her best to cope, often through significant, insurmountable family and societal challenges of the time. Madeline showed her love by *doing*, and in being steadfast through all family turmoil, no matter how daunting.

For over forty years, she kept Thoreau's quote "In Wildness is the preservation of the world." prominently posted in their home. Her intent is clearer to me now. I understand deeply that, in all their meanings, wildness and wilderness, both of spirit and of place, were part of and key to her own preservation.

These days, as I read her saved letters and writings, and page through her photos and memorabilia, mostly stored for years, unseen by us, I understand her as a different, benevolently "wilder" person from whom any of us thought she was. That probably happens to a lot of us regarding our parents after they are gone. Her dusty, randomly boxed written and photographic record of her long life suggests that Madeline was not at all the lonely, worn woman of the last few of her 93 years. Rather, she was an introspective yet gregarious person of amazing creative energy, whom I have come to admire and appreciate more fully. As a person, parent, and grandparent, she was emphatically more adept and astute than we were aware, and always alert to the world around her, human and natural. Aging took its toll on her, but it is evident how my own family and I owe considerably to her influence. We will continue to realize and comprehend that for the rest of our lives.

Examples of Maddy teaching us to engage and learn are far reaching and numerous. She introduced me to this little village in the tall pine forest, and to this cherished five acres of family land, when I was a small child. Madeline, along with my dad, sister, and me, "The Four Kings" they would say, camped here often, and spent so many days just down the road at her father's cabin and at Lucius Woods Park. I grew to love this quiet place from her and Grandpa Favell's influence. They later passed this property on to me. After Madeline's funeral in late June 2005, we reverently distributed some of her ashes in the ancient forest here, amidst several of the towering Norway pines she treasured. Her love for this land and forest kept us engaged here. Her love of place brought Debbi and I back to this centering, anchoring homestead to focus our lives when the time was right for us. We are so thankful.

Madeline always fostered my curiosity and thirst to know more. For example, in this new year of 2009, proclaimed the "Year of Science" (YOS), I am reminded of her enthusiasm fifty-two years ago, when I was seven, for the International Geophysical Year (IGY) in 1957-1958. She engaged with that global event as an interested citizen scientist and energetic advocate for science education. She and the IGY encouraged my life-long interest in science of all types, especially geology, earth sciences, and physics, influencing me toward science and education careers. I am sure her focus affected the lives and career pursuits of our sons, too; one now a physicist, the other a physician/biochemist.

Perhaps most importantly, Madeline taught me much of how to learn, and that learning about *anything* could be fun, a worthwhile, noble investment of life. Her wide-ranging intellectual impact was absorbed, and is still being lived out, by our today-family in the choices we have made and followed, as we explore the world, open to new ideas and unafraid of anyone's opinions. Her creativity and knowledge were vast.

As I recently, randomly watched a television special on the history of the French Revolution, I recalled Mom telling me of these same facts and stories when I was a small boy. The program covered things that were just as she had said, though I largely ignored her back then. At that time, it all went over my head; I never knew and did not appreciate her depth of knowledge and wisdom. Maybe that happens to a lot of us with our parents. My eyes are beginning to open now, as I am understanding more about Madeline and how she helped shape our lives. She knew so much, and was interested in everything. I know there is much more to learn of her life and recognize of her influence.

In a practical sense, this Tale is my written tribute, at last, to my under-appreciated mother. We didn't know her story. Madeline's innate humility and shyness kept her from sharing the background of her life when she could. I wish I could ask her more, and learn more from her.

A lesson for all of us from this is that we must tell our life stories now. Take time: *make time to* communicate with your family, kids, and grandkids while you can. They and you may think it is boring, repetitious, excessive information now. It is not. There will be a day sooner that you think when they'd like to speak with you about many things, and will not be able to. Talk now and get acquainted. Write it down now, while life and breath and memory are intact. Madeline's talent and enthusiasm for all of life are evident in her well-worn moccasins, safe in our drawer here now. But Madeline's moccasins can convey only part of her complex, unique story, so much of which we'll never know.

Shaped

Long-term care shapes a family. A short summary of this entire book could be that we are grateful for the difficult care experiences life has brought us. And now, we are so grateful for the freedom to return to our forestland of the Red Pump.

These Tales are naturally autobiographical. So, if you are to know my family and me, you must understand that, until June 2005, we have had at least one direct family member in long-term institutional care since 1950; all of my life. As brave and resolute as a person or family can try to be, years of being ever responsible for others, paying bills, and making the circuit to visit loved ones weekly, or when you can at various distant care units, all wear on you. Independence Day and Thanksgiving of 2005 marked the first holidays in my 55 years to that point in my own life during which I did not have direct family who were institutionalized. Those were the first holidays—ever—during which I didn't have to spend the days at county care units, hospitals, or nursing homes with family, plus traveling to and from those extended care sites.

That could sound harsh, I know. I surely don't mean it that way. My family members who needed extended care were not to blame; this essay is not an effort garner pity. They taught me so much. The insights and shaping I gained from all of those caring years made me who I am, and taught our whole growing family to deal with real life at early ages. This Tale serves only to narrate some of the wealth of experiences my family and I learned from our kin. Their long-term care tested and toughened us, and made us grow; it surely made me grow more than I can say. Life, time, and health nowadays, to live in a freer, happier way, are even more treasured for us because of those tests offered during such taxing, wearing years from which there seemed no elevation.

My own life experience with long-term institutional care of close loved ones and family has been extensive. Grandmother Inga lived much of her life with serious chronic health difficulties, then died at age 69 in 1953, when I was three. She was a brilliant woman, a genius scholar, musician and artist, I have been told by many. I read of her abilities in her many letters from friends, saved now in our family collection here. We find supporting records of her abilities in her writings, sheet music, letters, photos, and notes from friends, family, and many others of the early 20th century. My only sibling, Karen, was placed at the cloistered, private residential school because of her developmental disabilities when she was 13, also when I was three. My in-laws and my own parents thrived for long, full lives, but lived bravely with dementia, cancer, strokes, or other diseases of aging near the ends of their lives. Their prolonged periods of senescence extended from before 1985 through mid 2005. That became a challenging 20-plus year period of taking care of many loved ones, while in the midst of our sons' growing up, K-12 schooling, and hectic university years. We came to know long-term care too well.

We all grew from it, as we dealt with the long illnesses of loved ones, their deaths, and funerals in those years. My mother, Madeline, passed away on June 3, 2005, just as we were in the process of moving back to this family homestead she loved, here near the Red Pump. Until that day, every holiday of my life, and so many of the days in between, centered on travel to and from and time spent with these direct relatives who were in long-term institutional care around the state. Those 55 years were often long and sad, in between scarce, fleeting family joys.

Most people did not, do not, *cannot* understand. Debbi and our boys brought light in my own seemingly endless dark world of ongoing care and concern.

During one period from about 1997 to 2002, when our boys were in the midst of many once-in-a-lifetime active high school and university days and adventures which we wanted to share and savor with them, the demands of that long-term care intensified. It included having five individual family members, my sister, parents, and in-laws, in five different care institutions throughout west central Wisconsin simultaneously. It became nearly overwhelming at times. I marvel now at how we made it through those years, still largely intact physically and emotionally. It surely toughened us. My own role as always-concerned son, forbearing brother, legal guardian, power of attorney, and financial go-to person for so long, was well learned. It shaped my life in more ways than I can readily understand. Nonetheless, for all I gained, I would not wish it on anyone. Long-term care is grindingly tough on everyone in a family. Imagine multiplying that care times five...all at the same time.

Now, after more than a half century of the challenges, I miss the people very much. They shaped all of our lives. But I do not miss the never-ending difficulties. My prayer and fervent hope is this: Our tedious, trying days of being in the halls, waiting rooms, and confines of long-term behavioral-care and physical-care facilities, in the grasp and scrutiny of county and state bureaucrats, social workers, administrative operatives, and prying staff of all kinds; of paying bills, being examined constantly by social service agencies in person and on endless forms; of being in court and having family members' lives directed by attorneys and judges, may be done for a long, long while. I pray that will be true.

When I give thanks this and every year, it is for all the people and events who have shaped me; for the events that have challenged and daunted but not broken me, my wife, and sons for all these years. And I give thanks now also for the freedom to be more like many other people, who can be part of settings that are more uplifting. We do not always have to travel to care facilities now, putting on our smiles as we walk through those dark institutional front doors.

Chronic sorrow is the term I've heard professionals use to describe so much of this care-centered life we have lived. I am making a conscious and concerted effort now to live with and to express chronic, lasting *joy*, and looking forward to at least another 56 years of the latter. I am glad and relieved beyond measure to be here at last, building our decks and moving boulders into place near the Red Pump. There is nowhere else I'd rather or have to be. My family and I have been shaped. We are tired. But more so, we are thankful and glad.

Thanks . . . for the Failure?

Words and language guide our thinking. What we say and read, and what we hear in our heads, that internal language we each use to think, guides our thoughts and actions. Sometimes, while I mow or cut brush near the Red Pump, I think of these things, and they concern me. Have you noticed how language has changed? Here are just a few examples from our everyday lives.

It seems we now have to be politely grateful to clerks in stores for letting us buy things. Yes, I am sure you have seen it—or done it. We, the customers, now tend to thank the clerk, rather than the other way around. I grew up working in stores as a clerk or cashier, and was always taught to count out the change to the customer (another thing that has passed us by, I fear!). We were to then look at the buyer, and sincerely say, "Thank you!" You may even remember the "Thank you for shopping with us." campaign in some stores a few years ago, where clerks were actually penalized for not saying a phrase of that type.

When did this change? When did we all start thinking it was correct etiquette, even our polite social duty as consumers, to thank the business that just took our money? At a profit, no less. We made the effort to earn the money, to bring it to their store, to shop, select, and then pay for items. So why do we thank them? Words seem to have changed our thinking.

I did a bit of informal, unscientific research one weekend, and noted what happened when I bought things in six different stores in our area. As I went through the checkout lines, in all cases but one, the cashier simply handed the change or charge slip back to the buyer ahead of me.

In five of six cases, the customer said "Thank you," not the clerk. It was as if the store had just done the buyer a great favor. When it was my turn, I actually had to restrain myself from saying "Thank you" (it has almost become a habit), and to just wait for what the cashier said. One out of the six thanked me. The others simply handed me my change or receipt, and looked on to the next customer in line, with no words at all.

It seems words, language, and how we think when buying (or selling) things have indeed changed. Are we that grateful nowadays just to get *any* customer service, let alone courteous service, that we, in our uneasiness, must try to introduce at least some polite rhetoric to the situation by preemptively thanking each cashier?

Another language example: During the Olympics, as well as other local and national sporting and athletic events, we so often see and hear the word "failed". Someone failed in his or her bid to become the Olympic gold medalist; some team failed to win the World Series; and so on. The fact is they succeeded beyond most others in the world to get to that level of skill and competitiveness. They may not have won the top prize, but they have surely out-succeeded nearly everyone else on the planet.

This language-guided thought process of either total failure or total elite success, I submit, is bogus. It makes us believe that, unless we can be the absolute best at something, we shouldn't even try at all. I read one sports writer who even used the terms "contenders and pretenders" in referring to entrants in a local five-mile run. I completely disagree with this thinking. We who were *doing* the race were not pretending.

The success, the true victory in life, is in the effort, not in the trophy. And this concept becomes truer the longer we live. It is way better to be present, to be alive, active, and doing the walking, running, skiing, shooting hoops, golfing, passing the puck on the ice, biking, curling, or whatever else you like to do, while having fun and getting some great exercise and socializing, than to give up doing because you are not going to be the best.

When it comes to our own enjoyable, life-sustaining activities and exercise, perfection is never required. Participation is! Being active, at whatever level we can each muster, is vastly better than letting the receding goal of elite contention cause us to become a "couch slouch" (the preferred term now, I gather; not so pejorative toward potatoes). The real victory is in the doing, and in the keeping-on-doing all your life, not in the winning. Don't let anyone's words fool you.

In short, the words we hear, speak, read, and write shape our thinking. In some areas, such as those above, how we think needs to be rethought. Just a few thoughts from a guy working in the woods near an old Red Pump and some giant Norway and White pines that have lived through so many changes.

Winter Love

Winter is great, especially here in this land of the Red Pump. Why? Two words: No Bugs. Winter is also great because our barn turns into a huge walk-in cooler, so handy for all those special holiday and weekend leftovers and beverages, often from Halloween way through Easter. What fun to just walk in and grab from an assortment of cold treats off the shelves. Winter also adds constantly evolving three-dimensional sculpture to our rocks and logs around the Red Pump and throughout the forest. Our huge glacial erratic boulders scattered around become artists' dreams, always changing in light and form with the drifting, blowing snow.

Another huge reason I love winter is that ice and snow can make us, for a few months of the year at least, almost super human. We can slide faster, fly farther, and float smoother on our skis, skates, and sleds, under our own power and with just a little help from our friend gravity, than by self-powered methods at any other time of the year. Ice and snow give us each capabilities to move in ways we simply can't in other seasons. During winters around here, we all frequently, literally *walk on water*: the solid kind called lake ice. What a boost to our collective self-esteems!

I also love to ski--any type of skiing. I've tried them all, and this is my 57th year as a skier. My folks started me as a ski jumper when I was two, then I switched to downhill skiing when I was about age eight. Since then, I have raced a lot, been a Senior National Ski Patrolman, Patrol Director, Ski Instructor, and have shredded on snow boards. Plus, I've done much cross-country skiing and skijoring over the years--often, now, from right out our door at home in paradise, here in rural northwestern Wisconsin.

The primary reason I love winter, however, has become more evident to me as I see our grown sons living actively and dealing with life's challenges. We taught them early on to ski and race well. In slalom racing, if you fall, go off the race course, or "miss a gate", meaning you make a mistake and don't go through the pairs of red and blue poles according to race rules, you have two options: you can keep on skiing, hoping no race official notices and you don't DQ; that is, disqualify. Or you can stop, taking the time, effort, and embarrassment to climb back up the slope, and ski down through the gate the full, correct way. You lose the race, but you do what's right. When my wife and I coached our boys in racing, we always stressed how important it was to be persistent, honest, and to finish the full slalom course according to the rules, not just being concerned about finish times.

They learned well. As I watch them now in their young adult lives dealing with personal and professional challenges and frequently "climbing back" through the many metaphorical missed gates we all have in life, they have become *our* mentors. This life lesson they learned so early, and they now live out so well, has become the main reason I love winter.

So Whose Land Is It?

Land stewardship, and private versus public models for it, concerns us all. In Wisconsin and throughout the world, there are certain special places local people and others recognize as being different from and more unique than other land around them. These tracts may be forest, shoreline, wetland, farm field, prairies, or other properties. The Red Pump world here and this special piece of family forest are such places for our family. The question arises: Who cares better, more effectively, more efficiently for these special places we all treasure so? Are private or public owners better stewards?

Examples of effective, open, state ownership and stewardship of important lands include the North Shore of Minnesota. This is dramatic terrain along Lake Superior's beautiful coastline, all the way up to the Canadian border, south of Thunder Bay, Ontario. When the north coast of Minnesota was being settled by Europeans in the mid to late 1800s and early 1900s, some wise regional and state legislators and planners foresaw that these prime, unique, dramatic coast lands would be quickly and thoroughly staked out, literally, by wealthy private owners during those boom years. Visionary public officials foresaw that access to the rugged, awesome Lake Superior coast along the eastern border of Minnesota, once sold off to private owners, might well never be retrieved. Open, public access to and use of these lands could have been forevermore restricted because of the exclusive private ownership, and Lake Superior could have been cut off from the general populace in those areas.

Wisely, Minnesota power brokers of the time, both public and private, created many accessible, open, reasonably priced public access points. These took the form of state parks and other preserves that will remain in public hands for perpetuity. Developers or others who might harm or lessen their natural value and accessibility to all, we believe, can never buy out these properties. Never say never.

Minnesota parks and access points along Lake Superior remain well cared for, appreciated, even revered by so many from Minnesota, Wisconsin, Ontario, and all over the nation and world. And, again the good news: they remain fully usable for many purposes by anyone who can cover the small access fee charged by the state. This is a success story of public vs. private ownership of lands treasured by many.

On the other hand, we are aware in Wisconsin that other results are possible. This may be true as well in other states and provinces. When state or federal governments take over a locally-treasured piece of property, the exercise of eminent domain for other purposes (roads, power lines, airports, other invasive developments) seem more likely; invasive land uses have been more likely with public ownership in cases I have witnessed. Private owners, who for generations have treasured and stewarded a property, seem more assertive in its protection and fair use.

Private ownership of especially treasured lands, parks, water access points, and other properties has it advantages but certainly disadvantages too. Private ownership by individuals almost always translates into restricted access for others to the property, stream, lake, river, or waterfall. The public often loses freedom to roam and explore lands under private ownership.

So, switching viewpoints again: Responsible, informed, educated private owners, individuals or local communities over generations can come to deeply appreciate the many purposes, uniqueness, and sanctity of the property they steward. Many have shown they do a more cost-efficient stewarding, and protecting of that property than state, regional, or federal groups may do at a distance. I understand that these issues are complex and multifaceted, and that my ideas here can be construed as simplistic. No single solution or method applies to all cases of public vs. private ownership and stewardship of pristine, cherished lands, in this state or any other.

In general, however, I submit that private individuals, local owners and informed, cooperative, engaged communities who understand what they are conserving and using, will be better local eyes and ears to watch and guard essential lands than will more distant overseers and bureaucratic caretakers, no matter how well intentioned. Whenever possible, this is my assertion: Education is better than regulation. In an ideal sense, this applies to land ownership as well to all other areas of public and private policy. Back here, however, in the real world of rules and laws, and of northern Wisconsin, both models have merit and are situation dependent.

As the fifth generation stewards of our property (we are never really owners in terms of geologic time), we are pleased to thrive at and take care of this beautiful place during our so-short lifetimes and then pass on the stewardship role to others. We family members knew from early on in life that care of this property was one of our main life missions, and are now into our third century and second millennium of family members keeping this incredible tract of forest where we live as unspoiled, pristine, yet still available for others' appreciation as we can. This mission will pass to our sons, whom I know are ready to be the next generation of caregivers for this small but so unique, so beautiful piece of our planet. Perhaps that is the best kind of stewardship of land: by those who truly love it, be they private individuals or the informed, engaged, committed public stakeholders who treasure a place.

The best solutions to this greater issue vary from place to place, instance to instance. Trusting in those who daily live on and near these precious northland forests, prairies, and waters of our state is essential. Providing responsible education to help them in their land use and care is preferable to regulation. That is especially true, I assert, when well-meaning committees do regulation at a distance. Too often this may involve people for whom the land can become just another far away piece of ground to be administered.

These are some of my many woodland thoughts as we hike the trails everyday near our Red Pump, through these tall, tempered old pines, and amid the rich, diverse under-story plant world below them. You don't have to be a tree hugger like me to realize this incredible forest has been here a lot longer than we have or will be. It deserves our lasting respect.

Sounds Like Spring

March, April, and May are truly spring. We, who live in this forest near an old Red Pump, and near a still mostly wild lake, hear lots of new sounds during these months. And we have memories of human voices from springs past. Here are a few of my recollections. I'll bet you remember many others.

March. "The Blue Lines will melt by March 15," the volunteer hockey coach lamented, as we tried to practice more while there was still outdoor ice. Now we typically don't even have ice outside in March. "If March comes in like a lamb, it goes out like a lion." Or vice versa? I was never sure just what that meant. It seems March weather can be just about anything from 80 above to 20 below over the years. "Beware the Ides of March!" from Shakespeare's play *Julius Caesar.* We had to memorize all those quotes in high school. I wonder if kids still do? "March into Spring!" one of my teachers declared every year. Guess that was better than "Fall into Spring."

April. "April Fool!" I've heard of some interesting, elaborate pranks, most involving super glue or plastic wrap. Hmmm, not appropriate to describe here. "Happy Income Tax Day!" (Ha!) Don't think we'll ever hear that one. More like: "*Blankity-blank-blank* April 15!" "Spring forward; fall back." for time changes. A handy phrase, but who really understands daylight savings time anyway? "Happy Birthday, Debbi," for my wife who will always be the gorgeous 20 year old I fell in love with so many Aprils ago. I hope to say that to her at least a hundred more Aprils! Hey, you can hope…

May. "Happy May Day!" As little kids, we made construction paper May baskets in school. They had a loop handle and were filled with small candies. We were supposed to hang a basket on a girl's front door, ring the bell, and run. She had to chase you and kiss you if she caught you. As a seven year old, that thought terrified me. Sandy, our neighbor girl, hung a basket on my door one year, rang the bell, and ran. I knew it was she, and knew she could sprint faster than I could, so nothing developed. Nowadays, that May Day activity would likely get someone arrested. Times sure change. "Happy Mother's Day!" Thanks, Moms! For everything. We miss you. "Don't plant your garden until after Memorial Day because it'll freeze." So true. We've been nipped more than once by a late-May visit from Jack Frost. Best of all: "Happy Anniversary, Debbi!" May 24: still and always the happiest day of my life.

Importantly for May: "Remember Our Vets." On Memorial Day, we pause to remember all who have made this good life possible for us. "Thank you" is way too little to say. This would be a vastly different, immeasurably more difficult world were it not for the selfless service of those we honor and remember on Memorial Day.

And finally: "April showers bring May Flowers!" And what do May Flowers bring? Pilgrims, of course, bearing bad jokes. April also brings greening to the blueberry and lingonberry plants around our Red Pump and in our other rock gardens, as well as the rest of the forest.

Did June 'joy that? *May* we *Spring* on to the next chapter now?

Moccasin Mike Road, Melba, and MacGyver

One of our family heroes owned this land we treasure, for just a short time about a hundred years ago. Clough Gates, my great uncle through marriage, was quite a man who lived fully and contributed much to the Superior and Solon Springs areas, as well as to the state of Wisconsin.

It was the summer of 1954. The City of Superior, Wisconsin was celebrating its Centennial, and Uncle Cough (rhymes with *tuff*) was the energetic Chairman of the event. Super City; some of our family's home for so long, was 100 years old. Most of what I remember from the celebration itself is what I have seen in our family pictures. But I do recall vividly a few important (to a four-year old) events that penetrated even more deeply into my young brain.

First would be the steam engines and trains down at the old depot in Superior. The low, powerful vibrations and chug, chug, chug of the old-time steam engines as they moved the trains sink into your soul forever. Also, the loud, commanding whoosh and hiss, as the engines slowed and brought the trains to rest, are all unforgettable. I recall too the voluminous clouds of water vapor, and the intense heat coming off the engines as we watched them work from close by that bright, sunny summer day.

For some reason, I also recall in detail the long hand-tied bow tie that my Uncle Clough wore with his dapper suit for the occasion. He had let me, the eager young nerd-kid in plaid suspender shorts (good grief), "help" him tie his bow tie. Not much help, probably, but I can remember trying hard to keep the ends straight and to loop them correctly for him. Clough was my *de facto*, acting grandfather; I was honored. Tying my shoes at that time was challenge enough for me; it still is some days. So the Superior Centennial picture of him with his natty bow tie neatly and properly knotted likely had nothing to do with my efforts.

The downtown Superior events held are a bit foggy, figuratively only, to me now. But I sure remember the next part. We rode in Uncle Clough's and Aunt Mabel's big car out to Wisconsin Point on the then rough-graveled Moccasin Mike Road for a picnic with the whole family. They even had the wicker picnic basket of food, and the red plaid picnic blanket to put out on the beach for everyone.

Then two amazing things happened, based on my four-summers-old memory. The first was that we had Melba toast with the picnic lunch; the first time for me. I thought they were kidding when Aunt Mabel first handed it to me to eat. It seemed like just some dry, old, stale, hard bread. Today, we might even call it edible Styrofoam, or some such. Anyway, it seemed a pretty strange thing to eat.

But it was OK, I guess. I ate it. By the end of that busy day, I was really hungry, having not eaten much in the rush of events. That was probably why it tasted all right at the time. If, in fact, actual Styrofoam had been invented then, and we had had it with us, it may also have tasted fine to me at that point. Who knows?

The other amazing event I recall with complete clarity, and it will stay with me the rest of my life. As we drove in and out of the many side inlet roads (dirt tracks, actually) checking out the beach areas off Moccasin Mike Road, the huge, lumbering car bottomed out several times on the rocks, roots, and sand ruts we were driving over. We heard a clank -- and a crunch.

Soon, the smell of gasoline surrounded us. Uncle Clough's beautiful, bodacious Buick (maybe it was a big Oldsmobile?) had sprung a leak.

The gas tank was punctured. We could see and smell liquid draining from under the car onto the sand-rock-rut road we were on right near the Lake Superior shore.

Without missing a beat, and still dressed in his 1850s-period Centennial suit, and of course still wearing the bow tie with which I had assisted him, Uncle Clough popped two sticks of gum into his mouth. As a little kid, I thought that was pretty cool: immediate treats in an emergency still seems like a good idea.

He chewed the gum furiously for a few moments, then hurriedly bailed out of the driver's seat to his left and disappeared under the car. I had no idea what was going on. He emerged a couple minutes later, smiling broadly, then he drove us back to their house, with the gas tank fixed just fine...for a while, at least.

Years later, when I read "The Thinking Machine" books and stories in school in the 1960s, and then saw the "MacGyver" television series in the 1980s, all based on creative problem solving, I remembered Uncle Clough and our adventures that day. I have learned since how he helped socially engineer the world for good in many ways through his personal influence, and his professions of business and journalism. He did a lot for others in his city and state, often in his trademark creative, covert ways. Notably for us, he and Mabel housed and helped my mother for years, so she could earn her college degree in 1933 at Superior State Teachers' College, while her mother was hospitalized for years.

After he passed away, I also found out from family members and his neighbors how Clough had confidentially helped others to acquire much-needed dental care and dentures during depression times, when such treatments were limited and prohibitively expensive for many. His examples taught me well in myriad ways; I always relive a bit of that thought-evoking gas tank experience each time I see problems solved creatively. Thanks for the lessons and learning, Uncle Clough.

And I still keep a pack of gum handy in my Subaru dashboard, just in case. But no Melba toast, please. Melba toast should be confined to the ends of kayaks, for flotation only.

Karen's Swing

Yesterday, I walked near the forest swing I made for my sister Karen. It was suspended between two thick oak trees, just to the side of the Red Pump. She enjoyed her swing often, and appreciated that I rigged it for her; a special gift from me, her "big" brother.

The swing bar and ropes broke years ago, before Karen left on her voyage into eternity. But fragments of swing and memory remain. Looking at where the swing used to be reminded me that human stories of this land, some so joyful, some amazingly painful, are what last in our memories. The long-ago swing got me thinking about my hero, my first and best teacher, Karen.

Sometimes the heroes in our lives are people who so obviously fit the role. They are noticed by the many; the acclaim they gain is deserved and well recognized. I admire and applaud those astronaut, military, and sports heroes. But some heroes are not that way at all. They seldom get noticed, until too late. My sister Karen was such a hero.

Karen was born in Watertown, WI, in 1939, around the beginning of World War II. When she was about 18 months old, she developed a severe kidney infection. Our pharmacist father and store manager mother, who owned the drug store in our little town then, Elkhorn, WI, could not get the new antibiotic drugs she needed. The war caused many short supplies of medications. Karen was extremely ill, with a sustained high fever of 108 Fahrenheit for more than a week. She suffered damage to her brain and body from which she never fully recovered. Based on what I can tell from pictures and family accounts of the events, the infection changed Karen from a typically developing, adorable toddler girl into someone who was different and troubled all the rest of her brave, isolated, and often, tortured life.

Even with this rugged start in her life, Karen was like everyone else in so many ways. Our parents spoke often of all the many fun, good things that happened for Karen, too. They said she attended elementary school through all the grades. She won the Walworth County 5th Grade Spelling Bee, played clarinet in her junior high school band, kept pet angora rabbits, played with neighbors, rode her decorated bike in city and neighborhood parades, and even had a few girl and boy friends.

But in the middle of her seventh grade year, our parents later said, the principal marched her across the street to our home. He rang our front door bell, and told my mother they could not teach Karen anymore. "She's yours to handle now," they reported he said. Disabilities of learning, behavioral, and cognitive types lumped together then as "mental retardation" were not well understood in 1953 when this happened; they are still not well comprehended now as we'd like. Our parents did the best they could to handle Karen at home, and were always very kind and loving to her. But I was only three years old, and some of her severe behaviors toward me at that time made them fearful. Upon the advice of their physician and family members, they entered Karen into a costly, private residential school for handicapped and "mentally retarded" children in far southern Wisconsin.

Our family, the three of us now, moved back to the home country in northwestern Wisconsin soon after. In 1955, that was a long way from her new school/home then, with no four-lane freeways, only slow two-lane rural roads, through so many little towns that suddenly lay between our close family members. It was hard for Karen and all of us. From a five-year-old's perspective, I will never forget the long, frequent, boring, and sad 500-plus mile round trips to and from that far place. Trips south were grueling, dangerous, and difficult for all the family to endure several times every year; the trips became much less frequent with the next passing years. Our long treks to see Karen also became more and more tediousness as the wear of repeated travel set in for us. Even as a little boy then, I understood how much Karen looked forward to, indeed, lived for coming home any time she could. That place was never a good location or home for her, but our parents did the best they could for her at the time and for the circumstances that applied.

At age 26, Karen was again spontaneously, capriciously it seemed, dismissed back to her home by the institution's administrators; exited from that distant southern residential school because she was too old, too recalcitrant. There was no prior notice, preparation, or foreshadowing for her or us. She had been there 13 years, and was coming home, immediately, now with significant behavioral difficulties, to instantly take up her new life in our small, rural town; not a good thing for Karen or anyone. Our parents worked hard, striving to make the abrupt transition with her, and to reconstruct bearable lives for all of us. I was a self-conscious, self-absorbed teenager, and the neighbors watched. What a combination for that hard time. Our parents' fortitude and tenacity are more incredible in retrospect each time I consider the complexity and anguish they juggled for our family.

Karen's behaviors and difficulties became more extreme, and were not her fault. Soon her life was a constant string of movings; in and out, in and out of county and state mental hospitals and care facilities. These included some disgustingly filthy nursing homes, and some locked-down, scary "psych wards" that looked, sounded, and smelled like something out of a bad horror movie. She existed that way, in those surroundings, most of the rest of her life, with just occasional glimpses of joy and sunlight, then steep drops back into despair for her, and for all of us in her family. Daily, we felt it, lived it, and were shaped by it. The careening roller coaster never stopped. I was trying to grow up during all of this and have a life, career, and family, and often felt sorry for myself. But my heart and thoughts were constantly with Karen, too, trying to imagine yet block out what she must have been enduring while I got to do all the good stuff of life. In many ways, I have always tried to live and achieve for both of us.

In 1972, I met Debbi; still and always my brightest star in the universe. She was the girl I loved, and whom I would marry in 1975. We made many plans. Most incredibly, Debbi took on my lifetime concern for Karen. In fact, through all of this, I have found one sure way you can tell if your new bride really loves you and is dedicated to her new family...really. It is this: Have your family church wedding in rural west central Wisconsin, then after the reception, immediately drive 200 miles south to the Mendota State Mental Hospital, the really far away and daunting one, in Madison, to visit your only sister. My new bride, Debbi, also my super hero forever, actively supported this so we could spend at least an hour or so with Karen on our special day of celebration. Karen was too ill, too agitated to be at our ceremony; we did our best to include her in our own way. It was the best, most loving thing we could do for Karen on that day, and I believe she understood that. Debbi made it happen. I will always be grateful.

Years passed. Karen and our family dealt with her and our dear others' mental and physical health crises, and their complex long-term-care challenges. Karen nearly died in 1976 from severe kidney problems brought on by her antipsychotic medications. We prayed earnestly for and rejoiced in her recovery from that episode, only to see it reoccur in her life. The original kidney damage haunted her, and our parents always profoundly regretted that they could not have helped her with the medications she needed when she was so little and vulnerable.

When Karen was about 59 years old, around 1998 (my age now as I write this), we learned she was in end-stage renal failure. Her weakened kidneys had processed many lithium-based and other drugs, and were now giving out. She received palliative treatments and medications, but she eventually was informed there was no cure. For a while, Karen considered kidney dialysis and toured a clinic unit, but she maturely and rationally decided that was not for her. For a brief time, I thought of myself as a possible kidney donor for her, though we didn't know if we matched. We carefully considered that possibility, but decided that, with my wife, young children, and new career, I needed to place my priorities with them, not with my sister. That was hard. Karen had nothing at that time but declining health and the promise of certain death. I still am not sure that we made the right decisions. We all did what we thought best in the situation at that time.

Karen and I spoke deeply together in September 1999, one of our best talks ever. She told me she was ready to die. She said she would just let her body take its course, and asked me to pray for her, remember her, and to play one of my instrumental music co-creations, "Celestial Sands" for her service as her special funeral song. Karen passed away peacefully at about 6 am on Sunday, September 10, 2000. The early morning phone call, from staff at her fine, nurturing last home in Hudson, stunned and shocked me, even though I thought I was braced for the inevitability of it all. Her tough life was at an end. It came so quickly. I never truly said goodbye.

We planned her funeral and memorial services for the next Friday afternoon in Eau Claire at Hope United Methodist Church. An amazing, wonderful number of her friends, family, care staff, and others she knew for many years—yes, fans, you could say--came to honor their beloved Karen. Her words, spirit, and toughness were celebrated; she had touched and buoyed the lives of many even in the midst of all her challenges. They recognized and knew that better than I did then. Karen taught them, and was their hero, no question. I at last began to more fully realize how much I had learned from her, and how much I respected and loved her; my big sister hero, Karen, our brave mentor.

In those last years, and throughout all our shared sibling times together, Karen taught me through her resolute, tumultuous life. She was my first and best teacher of the important, lasting things in life. Karen still teaches me as I reflect on her bravery, courage, and resolve to face alone the sad, terrifying changes she experienced in nearly all of her life; changes and challenges which escalated far beyond her own control and understanding. Karen was never a monster; she was my sister and my friend, whom I loved. Her differences were not of her doing, ever, and she did the best she could with what she had in her life. How frightened and how depressed she must have been through all those isolated years she lived, trying to be courageous…and I didn't always see it. In all the days I knew Karen, she never once spoke of taking her own life. I wonder how many of us could do the same. After all else she had lived through and taught me, Karen's quiet acceptance of her certain death that early September morning confirms her, forever, as my hero.

At her memorial service, I played as well as I could that day, offering my music as prayer, and as a tribute to her. Weeks later, I went alone with our pastor to the cemetery in Menomonie, where I placed Karen's small wooden box of ashes in the dry autumn ground by hand, by myself, as the minister read scripture verses in her memory and honor. That was my last act of loving care for my sister. It now seems so minimal for the hero whom I took so long to notice. Karen, my first and best teacher, saved and enriched my life in times and ways she never knew. I am still discovering those ways now.

Although the heavy, thick log top bar and the old ropes of Karen's forest swing weathered, broke, and fell years ago, I will rebuild it all soon; this summer, I hope. Karen would like that. New life is coming.

Blueberry Moose

Several times each year, my demure wife, Debbi, transforms into an exhaustingly efficient, forest-cruising, long-striding, berry-picking Blueberry Moose. I can't keep up. And you should see her in the rest of her life, beyond gregarious fruit and vegetable gatherer. There is much to say about Debbi, my best forest friend and love of loves, and our boys' adventure mom. Let's start at the beginning of our shared story.

Debbi and I made our first northland trip together on January 2, 1974, two days after our first official evening "date" as a couple that New Year's night. We both lived in the Eau Claire area then, having known each other for years as ski buddies and hiking friends. I told her of our old family farm in northern Wisconsin, but she had never been here. She had yet to experience the Red Pump and the pure water from this deep glacial ground moraine. Although, as a young girl, Debbi had briefly traveled through Duluth and northern Minnesota into Ontario, the northland was mostly new adventure territory to her on our first trip together. Once we got here, Debbi knew she fit right in.

We first visited Solon Springs and "Cozy Cove", originally Grandpa Favell's retirement log cabin, on the southwestern shore of Upper St. Croix Lake. It was built in 1950, on some of the family homestead land from around 1880-1890, just down the gravel road from this forest we call home. Doc Favell passed on in 1964 at age 93, and our family sold Grandpa's beloved lake-cove cabin and surrounding property later that year. The new folks, the Stewarts, remodeled his small dwelling, living in the cabin and its expansion for years.

On New Year's Eve, 1974, in that sub-zero January midnight, their home burned to the ground. This happened, we later learned, just as

Debbi and I were preparing for our epic first drive north to visit these friends. Their family all got out safely, but the cabin was destroyed by the fire, and by the necessary emergency efforts of the fire department. Cozy Cove, cabin site of so many of my boyhood memories and fun days, lay scattered and demolished there as charred, sawed, two-foot log sections; still-smoldering rubble now on frigid snow, soot and char-blackened chunks starkly contrasting with pristine white below.

Debbi and I were stunned. We were grateful for the safety of our friends, and also for our renewed acquaintance with them. But why under such terrible circumstances? She and I now understand the numbing shock of this loss as an early personal precursor to the many challenges we would face in our lives together. Our trip continued up Highway 61 along the Minnesota north coast to Ontario, to visit other best friends, the Powlowskis. Our travels were a dream fulfilled for us, and we got better acquainted in our first northland days together.

Debbi passed muster on all counts with these close folks, we heard years later. With their nod and that of our parents, and a lot of other life changes, the stage was set for our engagement in August 1974, and our marriage on May 24, 1975. We soon moved to Superior in July, and began enjoying the northland together for a lifetime. As I write this, it is January 2009, and we are in our 34th year of married fun. All is well at the Red Pump. We are convinced this definitely will be a long-term affair.

As we lived and learned as northlanders, my energetic, versatile mate began her seasonal morphing into Blueberry Moose, an often dramatic, sudden transformation. When wild blueberries are out in early July, so is Debbi, stalking them from the back gravel roads we drive together. She spots a patch of blue, determinedly hikes in, and soon has bowls of fresh wild blueberries in her keep. You can virtually see her sprout long moose legs, sharp eyes, and perky ears each year to target these tasty treasures. I soon learned all I can do is pick along side her as best I can, with my slower fumble-fingered pace, while she forages our year's supply of bucket after bucket of blueberries to freeze and make into pies, breads, and muffins. No stopping a determined, mission-driven Blueberry Moose on the loose, and not only for blueberries. Debbi's lycanthropic shift happens each and any time other nuts, vegetables, and fruits become ripe. Wild strawberries, plums, raspberries, blackberries, hazelnuts, apples, and of course garden-grown squash and pumpkins, you name it. All are subject to her aggressive vegetable predation.

That mystical, wonderful transforming of Debbi continues. It is based within her numerous prior years of picking berries as a then unlabeled, yet undesignated youth Moose; it persists even now into her highly-mature (?) adult days. Indeed, it has intensified. We have no grandchildren yet, but I can envision the pace she'll set for them if we do. Their picking apprenticeships will be fast and thorough: blueberry Mooselets stalking the forest and fields in all seasons, taught and trekked well by Master Mother Moose, Debra.

Debbi has always been an adventurer, and not just for food. From her many leaps off her family's farm windmill tower and barn, to her years of playing 4H softball, especially catcher on the men's team, to her diligence and creativity to win 4H sewing awards and trips to the Wisconsin State Fair representing her county in 4H competitions, to her many years working on the family dairy farm, and through her many part-time jobs while putting herself through university, she has been a trouper. She earned her master's degree (all 4.0 work) in adult education, specifically *andragogy*, adult learning, while our two sons were in their early teen years, and during periods of intense care of family elders. One tough woman, that Debra.

My mother and father loved Debbi. They recognized right away all she brought to our family. One early, dramatic sign we knew made her special was Debbi's legendary canyon somersault. My dad, Victor, Debbi, and I were hiking in a beautiful wild area west of Menomonie, called "Paradise Valley", a unique, narrow sedimentary-rock canyon carved by an ancient meandering stream. On hot summer days, we often wandered and wondered our way through the echoing labyrinthine stone hallways, hiking on the central rocky streambed.

On this particular day, Debbi was walking the upper canyon bank to our right and north, as Dad and I walked the cobbled stream gravel below. It was mid summer, and the cool comfort of the rock walls and rippling water was needed on that scorching day. Debbi hiked quietly, just above us about 15 feet on the forested rim of the canyon wall. Without saying a word, and with no prior indication to us, she walked over to the edge of the canyon. We watched as Debbi dropped her shoulders and head into flight, tucked her legs, and two-footed an agile landing on the moist, soft sandy streambed next to us, avoiding the rocks. She did a flawless feet-to-feet flip from the top of the wall down to us, got in step, and kept on walking. You may think I'm making this up. I'm not.

Dad and I were impressed. We accepted it as something Debbi would likely do at anytime. As we all thought about and discussed this later, it turned out she had not planned to be the spontaneous acrobat, but had simply gotten too close to the edge, and was trying to make the best, reflexively, of what could have been a disastrous fall. She pulled it off perfectly. Voyageur Victor and son took due note of this. We had a feeling this superhero gal was special.

Debbi's canyon flip set a tone for our northern adventures. Washing our hair under the frigid Red Pump water flow the first time was a jolt. I pumped while Debbi grabbed the shampoo and washed, rinsed, and repeated. She said her head was absolutely numb from the cold water. She pumped for me, and I found the same. Our camp outdoor thermometer measured the pump water, from 126 feet down, at 42 degrees Fahrenheit. No wonder our scalps were without feeling.

When our boys came along in a few years, Debbi initiated them into hand and head washing under the pump. Other firsts occurred for us around the Red Pump. Adam, at about age 15 months, had his first drink of ginger ale from Mom as we picnicked with family near the pump in summer, 1980. He needed a cold-water "chaser" to get the grimace off his face as he reacted to the bubbles and tartness of the pop. Seth, in summer 1981, at about age 8 months, was toddling with Mom near the pump, when he tripped and fell onto a short, mowed-off raspberry bramble, cutting his left eye lid deeply. We whisked him into the Superior hospital emergency room, where he had stitches, one of three repairs to that eyebrow and lid before he was three years old. He was becoming an adventurer just like his mom. We fretted that folks at our local ER were watching us as we kept bringing that same kid back with injuries to that same part of his body. Debbi grew alert to concerns, but kept on donating her blood at the same hospital, in the gallons total.

As a side note, if you were in charge of designating the blood type for my generous, always-upbeat Blueberry Moose wife, which would you choose? B-Positive, of course. In fact, that is her blood type, and the guiding theme of Debbi's life: Be Positive. It sure seems specially planned by Someone.

In one of those young summers, when our boys were still in car booster seats, Debbi was working to earn her second-degree black belt rank in karate. Her additional cross-training event was distance swimming, chosen because it presented a true challenge for her, and an opportunity to focus on improving important physical and mental skills other than those directly related to her empty-hand martial art, in which she had become so skilled over her many years of practice. On the day we started out from shore for Debbi to swim from the west lake bank near Cozy Cove over to the south end of Crownhart Island and back, about a half-mile or a bit more round trip, we did it as a family. Our toddler boys were each strapped in their booster seats in our seventeen-foot canoe, with their life jackets firmly tied on. I was in the stern; life jack fastened well, and with another one at my feet to throw to Debbi immediately if she needed it during her long lake swim.

We paddled out from shore about 30 feet as Debbi waded in, got to deep water, and started swimming. She had progressed only a few full, powerful strokes when she passed through some dense "musky weeds", and panicked. She excitedly swam up to the edge of our bobbing canoe, hung both arms over the left gunwale, rocking and nearly turning us over. There I was, her loving and admiring husband (the husband, no less, of a black belt mom trying hard to earn part of her next higher karate rank) poking and prodding her with my paddle to keep her from drowning her children. I pushed her off the boat, yelling, "Let go! You're going to swamp us!" Debbi gained her composure instantly, let go of the boat, and swam determinedly along side the canoe as we stroked to and from the island. It all took only about 30 minutes total for her, with just a few minutes of brief rests floating on her back as needed. Not bad for a recently non-swimmer adventure Moose. She and we were relieved to get back to land, pack up our canoe and boys, and hike back to camp, mission well accomplished. If only we had pictures.

Our intrepid swimmer and berry-harvesting Mama Moose is also a leading bug magnet. If there is a mosquito or tick within range of our outdoor world, it will find Debbi. She just deals with it. I regard it as a compliment to her, and figure they, too, sense how unique she is. They want to get in on the palpable *be-positiveness* that exudes from her. Mosquitoes in our tents, ticks in our many trailers over the years, and now beetles in our compact, earth-friendly home here, all find *her* first; they are drawn to Debbi. Actually, that seems true for all critters, human and other.

On a warm day in May, 2002, our 27th anniversary no less, we were avoiding black flies and mosquitoes, enjoying open lake scenery and new leaves in the surrounding forests, as we paddled our kayaks south on Upper St. Croix Lake. We explored creeks and shallows near the river entry for hours. As we paddled back to Kingswood, about midway on the south section of lake, we watched high above us as two bald eagles swooped and soared over us. They were so far up we could barely see them, still a common sight here, fortunately. But then, they joined talons high above, and fell, spiraling around each other, dropping fast now from 300 feet up, toward the water. Just as they neared the lake's surface, they parted their grasp, and each flew upward, arcing to their previous altitude in smooth, perfect formation. We were delighted and awed, having just witnessed "The Dalliance of the Eagles" as spoken of in poetry by Walt Whitman. To us, their performance represented renewed partnership, and was the eagles' "courtship ritual" we had seen and read about in the anniversary card we gave each other a year or two before. It was astounding, something we had never seen live, and precisely on cue as we came home from our anniversary kayak trip that afternoon. The eagles celebrated the joy and permanence of their relationship as we celebrated ours.

How appropriate and wonderful on that clear blue day in May. We learned later that Whitman may not have known he likely saw male eagles in this paired gravity dance, but we decided that was fine. Unlike the eagles, our anniversary "plunge" would be more figurative than literal, anyway. And unlike the eagles, we had to paddle hard as we headed back to camp for wine. Not that Debbi wouldn't have tried an aerial drop if she'd had the chance…hmm.

All her life, Debbi has been a true, enthusiastic adventurer. Through berry-picking marathons with my Dad, and many with me and the boys, to camping and hiking Isle Royale and skiing other forest paradises, to just living joyfully each day at home, she has an animated, pleasantly-wild explorer's spirit we know is part Moose, undoubtedly part Bear. I can even now visualize her placidly picking ticks, small and large, off our young boys as we gathered blueberries in 1981, keeping going, and telling them to keep playing, never thinking of Lyme disease or other tick borne illnesses, which, incidentally, we never got. She was destined divinely to be a "Boy Mom" she says, always looking for the fun and adventure of each situation, and never dwelling on danger or negatives.

There is much more to tell of Debbi's modern, creative, yet pioneer-brilliant and tough ways, which many people nowadays can't appreciate. My favorite tale crystallizes the simplest, yet perhaps best life example Debbi has passed on to all of us: When our boys were very little, we had kitchen stools at a simple curved counter in our Superior home. The guys would climb up and sit on the stools, bracing on the counter top. Quite often, they would fall off, landing on the tile floor or the carpet, sometimes banging painfully hard against the wrought iron railing around our open descending stairway near the kitchen. She'd carefully watch them for danger, of course, never overreacting. She'd just say, "Did you have a good ride?" They would generally smile, laugh, and say "Yeah!"

The good rides continue, as our multi-skilled morphing Moose leads us. Debbi's love, enthusiasm, and positive view of her family, and of this always-fascinating world, are interwoven into us forever. She changes those she touches, helping us see the richness and fun in every moment of life. Debbi is our berry-picking, front-flipping, mosquito-attracting, B-positive Blueberry Moose, who cares for us with all her being. Each day with Debbi is high adventure.

Children of A Lesser Doc

Health care providers are many and various. And there are definite pecking orders in the "What-kind-of-doctor-are-you?" food chain. My sons and I, it seems, are all children of a Lesser Doc.

To vastly oversimplify, my premise is that holders of the MD, Medical Doctor, the most familiar of US medical degrees, top the food chain. Neurosurgeons, cardiac, and orthopedic surgeons likely reside at the pinnacle of that Top-Doc pecking order. Within this descending MD lineage are other surgical specialists of all types, then general surgeons, and then other MDs who practice medicine but not surgery. Internists, psychiatrists, hematologists, among others, may be in that group. US-based culture now seems to place the general practice and family practice MD physician near the bottom of this top section of the Doc hierarchy. Other nations and cultures may view and value medical practitioners' degrees and related titles differently.

The next grouping of Docs in US public opinion, I submit, are holders of the DO, Doctor of Osteopathy, a degree that attracts less media popularization and thus less public familiarity. Doctor of Osteopathy (DO) is a common but still not well-known medical degree in the US. Do you know of TV shows titled "Makeus Wellerbe, DO" or online sites named "WebDO"? No, I don't either. Nonetheless, DO physicians of all specializations *are real doctors,* yes, offering valuable perspective; an osteopathic view of medicine instead of the allopathic bent of the MD world. DO Docs practice in the usual physician roles and specialties to which we are accustomed, depending upon their training and licensure, from neurosurgeon to family practitioner. But somehow, DO Docs don't seem to get the wider respect MD Docs do.

In Solon Springs, my grandfather, Ernest John Favell, DO, was a family practice physician and artist. He retired to his log cabin on the lake here, and, for a while, he owned this family forestland of the Red Pump. Some would consider Grandpa "Doc" Favell, DO, a Lesser Doc.

Following the Docs of MD and DO kinds, in order, could be the other surgical and invasive-procedure doctors who poke, prod, cut, drill, and stitch us, as well as treat using medications in their practices. These are oral surgeons, dentists, podiatrists, veterinarians, and other essential clinicians. I would also list chiropractors, optometrists, and audiologists in this group of doctors who test, touch, treat, medicate, operate, rehabilitate, and/or prescribe, for us and our family members of all species, with skill, knowledge, professionalism, and merit. Often, popular culture says these healing professionals are not "real" doctors.

Next in this regression of health care providers toward the even Lesser Docs, may be those Docs who, according to some TV wisdom, "can't really do you any good". These could be Doctor of Philosophy, Doctor of Education, Doctor of Science, Doctor of Psychology degree holders, and other similarly-degreed health professionals across a variety of "softer" fields; typically areas of highly-specialized, though largely non-invasive, clinical practice. Although these Docs are most often reliably well-educated products of grueling, difficult academic and clinical programs, internships, residencies, and post-doctoral training, they too often may be regarded as almost comedic by popular culture.

So, our sons and I are all children or (great) grandchildren of a Lesser Doc: an Ed. D. father and a DO (great) grandfather. Somehow we seem to have managed, even in our lowly status.

Curious isn't it that the term "doctor" derives from the Latin word, *docere,* meaning *to teach*, and that the "physician-as-doctor" concept developed from the learned academic degrees of the medieval church. It is also interesting that surgeons and dentists were once considered mere technicians, indeed barbers and bleeders in the former case. As I recall, university education for US physicians only became mandatory around the early 20th century, existing as an apprenticeship field prior to that pivotal time of development in medicine.

It makes you kind of wonder who the real doctors are. If educating patients for effective, curative change is truly at the root meaning of being a doctor, how many detached, uncaring physicians and others who bear that venerable title may actually be the Lesser Docs?

Ice Lemon

Upper Lake St. Croix was a frozen mirror on December 9, 2006. It was already 3 pm that sunny, cold day, and I knew the light would fade soon. At this latitude in December, we have usable sunlight for lake skating only until about 5 pm, depending on cloud cover. I finished my work for the day, and decided a long-distance skate on our seven-mile lake would be perfect. The lake ice here had frozen and firmed up a week before, and I checked it for safety earlier that day. No snow had fallen that late autumn, so the lake surface was a brilliant sheet of wide-open, clean ice; an old hockey player's private paradise, something rarely seen now in years of warmer winters.

From our garage hockey equipment box, I grabbed my Bauer skates, hockey gloves, and one of my old banged-up, ragged-taped sticks. Hadn't used them in a year or more, and it sure felt good to be heading for a well-lit skate on the glassy lake. With the total lack of snow in our area that year, the walk down to the lake bank was quick. There, I sat on a big rock at the edge, tied on my skates, and put on my gloves. I grabbed my stick, pushed off with my life-long skater's legs, and power glided out on my smooth, personally reserved rink. There was no one else around. It felt sublime to stride strongly, and skim over the slick, bright surface in the sun. I skated north about two miles in just a few minutes, where the ice got rougher, then I turned around and headed back south to explore around the Island at the other end of the lake.

In my rush to get out on the ice during sunlight, I forgot to bring a puck along to stick handle and pass as I skated up and down the lake. Our puck bag, of many black, hard rubber discs and a few red-plastic street hockey balls, was underneath other gear in our box. I neglected to grab it when I left. Not a problem for us old-time outdoor hockey guys; I just skated around any loose chunk of ice, small stick, or pine cone I saw on the ice, scooped it in with my curved stick, and passed it on ahead to my imaginary team mates as I skated hard. What fun, and what pure joy, to move nearly silently and effortlessly on a fast, friction free surface. "Best skate ever," I thought, even though I was alone on the lake. I skated along briskly, enjoying the wind from my speed, the endless blue sky, and the open panorama of the lake and surrounding forests. I was lost in my own exceptional early winter world.

Hey, up ahead, a dot on the ice. I skated up closer, and could see it was a faded yellow round thing. A tennis ball? Or had someone lost their street hockey ball or their driveway puck out here earlier? Curious, I charged up closer, never guessing from a distance what it really was: a whole lemon, frozen solid. How random: a loose lemon lying on the ice, hard as a rock, and faded from a bright grocery store yellow. The story behind that was anyone's guess. Maybe it fell out of an ice fisherman's cooler? Maybe animals got it out of garbage near a lakeshore cabin?

Who knows? Whatever its method of arrival on the lake, the lemon was exactly the missing "puck" I needed. I skated fast now, in rapid bursts, and slapped it on ahead on the smooth ice, then raced to catch up to it. I stick handled it forward and backward, in tight turns and long loops; I tried crazy behind-the-back and between-the-skates passes. They all worked; I was so loose and relaxed. My team of one was looking good. If only I'd had a partner to pass to or been in a game that day, could I have shown them my old stuff. I didn't even have to worry about hitting ruts or holes during all my gyrations, because the surface was so clean and clear; almost like newly re-iced indoor skating.

In awhile, I was tired from all my tight turns, stops, and reversals of directions with my new lemon puck. It was my first skate of the winter, so to slow it down a bit, I skated directly north, around the east side of Crownhart Island, then turned south at the Island's northernmost tip to skate along the sunny west shoreline in the windbreak of the tall pines on the Island. I cruised in a silent, pure world now, sending my ice lemon way out ahead of me, then chasing it, and shooting it out again, over and over.

My attention had been fully occupied for the last hour, up and down the lake, back and forth. Now, suddenly, a moving shape came into peripheral view over my left shoulder, something moving casually, at about shoulder height and maybe just ten feet now to my left. It was a large bald eagle coming slowly to my level, in full-spread glide pattern with wings at least seven feet across, tip to tip. He, maybe she, floated in silently, about five feet off the ice, focused on the lemon out ahead of us about fifty feet. The eagle held his glide pattern over the lemon, dropping to about three feet above the ice, then tipped his head down to look more closely at the yellow treasure as he passed above. He gritted through a tight left banking power turn, not unlike what I had been doing on the ice surface. Then he rose in the air, flew back around me, and came in again from north to south over the ice at about waist height, trying to get a closer look at this mysterious object.

I stopped and watched in amazement. My silent lake partner repeated his close airborne inspections of the random thing on the ice at least three more times, trying to figure out what that wobbling, flopping, skidding, yellow object was: Food, fish, unusual prey? I can only wonder. Then he flew off, disappearing in to the endless blue over the distant forests.

For a few moments, the Eagle and I were in a sunlit, clear world of curiosity that day on the ice. We shared our joy of moving freely and effortlessly: him reveling in gliding, swooping, and turning in the air; me enjoying much the same on my glassy two-dimensional medium of polished, once-in-a-lifetime lake ice.

We both pursued a silly target that afternoon, and had some fun together. I will never forget us both chasing that random lemon during on our shared St. Croix ice mirror adventure. What an experience, and what a story. I couldn't make it up if I tried. And, by the way, our ice lemon is still in a plastic bag in our barn freezer near the Red Pump to this day. It will stay there as a reminder of that cold afternoon of crystalline perfection, frozen fondly in my memory, forever.

Grandpa Gideon's Walk

We stay in motion here. It seems to be in our blood. We hike, run, ski, skate, or snowshoe at least 700 to 1,000 miles a year, covering two or three miles most days; many days much more. In rounded terms, that could be 350 X 3 = 1,050 miles...or more. Actually, this is fairly easy to accomplish because we do just a bit each day, and try to never over do. Our trekking spirit, in all its manifestations, came from somewhere. Grandpa Gideon King was surely one of the sources.

Gideon Roi (*King* in Canadian French), my father's father, came to Hayward, from rural St. Alphonse, Quebec, around 1880. Immigrants from French Canada and other northern countries moved to Wisconsin and Minnesota to work in the growing logging and timber industries of that time. Gideon was a gritty, rugged man, and a purposeful, powerful trail walker.

According to several sharp older family members, from whom we have heard these stories over many years, Grandpa Gideon hiked the woodland "Indian trails" from his small farm near Rice Lake to Menomonie, WI, and back. He did these walks in his fifth and sixth decades of life, once or twice per year as recently as 1908 to 1914. Grandpa Gideon walked at least 50 miles each way, completing the round trip in two days, we've been told, depending on the load he carried. At the water-powered grain mill on the Red Cedar River near Menomonie, he picked up and carried home essential sacks of flour or feed on his shoulders. He hiked them back to his family's small hand-built home and rock-strewn farm east of Rice Lake, just off County Highway C. My father, Victor, and his older sisters also described how Gideon built the barn there without nails, just wood pegs and timber framing. He also taught my dad to ski on their little hill in that yard, around 1910, using barrel staves with leather toe straps. Remnants of their farm still exist, near the Ice Age Trail system and just down the road from the Blue Hills Trails and Hardscrabble Ski Area, where four generations of our family have skied, learning to love skiing at young ages…and using modern gear.

Our family elders often told of how Gideon did his trail walks, as a simple matter of their lives then, dressed in his usual logger or farmer clothes and boots, and with no fanfare. It was part of survival for them at that time. He passed away in 1916 at age 61, leaving many stories of his woodsman's life that have been passed on by his children and wife. We believe these story snapshots to be plausible portions of King family lore, and are likely true as presented below. In any case, they are good summary yarns of northwestern Wisconsin life, values, and adventures at that time, and are worth preserving. Brief versions of a few of the many Grandpa Gideon tales include:

● In the 1880s, Gideon owned a small eatery and bar in Hayward, "The Stopping Place". His want ad for a new cook, placed in the St. Paul Pioneer Press, was seen by a 21 year old farm girl from Regensburg, Germany: Magdalena (Lena) Hetzenekkar. She soon moved here to logging-central northwestern Wisconsin to take the job, becoming Gideon's hard-working, strong, very smart cook, second wife, and my grandmother. Gideon's first wife, Ella, an Ojibwa-Metis woman from LCO Reservation, died early in life. They had four children.

● Gideon named his second son with Lena, "Henry". They had a total of seven children, five of whom survived to adulthood. Henry drowned at age 14 in Rice Lake as he tried to rescue a boy who had fallen in among the logs of a large floating jam from which they were swimming. Gideon gave his last new infant son, my father Victor, the middle name Henry, in honor of their lost son and brother. My dad often talked of brother Henry's story, and was always respectfully careful around water, whether swimming, canoeing, boating, or fishing.

●Around 1900, the City of Rice Lake rigged a tightrope high across the Red Cedar River just below the dam, over the rushing, swirling waters. Gideon walked end-to-end across the rope, bare footed, or with just his logger's wool socks on his feet. He'd fake a fall or two in the middle, maybe lose a sock, then grab the rope, climb back on again, and calmly complete his walk over and back. Fourth of July holiday crowds loved it.

●Gideon, though agile and strong, became a dedicated drinker by mid-life. When he was in town from the logging camps and ran out of money in the bars, he would pull his old red bandanna from his back pocket, spread it out fully on the barroom floor, and do a feet-to-feet flip forward then backward, in his logging boots, for drinks bought by admiring patrons eager to see him do it again and again.

●As a "jammer", Grandpa Gideon rode the rivers standing on top of floating log jams, balancing skillfully on the round, wet, always-moving crush of wood beneath him. He used a "pike" with wooden handle and steel point to free up logs as they floated down river, and to separate logs by company of ownership for their accounting and figuring payment. Gideon was never injured in his work, and he never knew how to swim.

●Gideon spoke Canadian French. Lena spoke German. They both insisted that they and their children speak, read, and write only

American English, their new family language in their new country. According to my dad's memories of when he was young, his father Gideon lovingly referred to him as *"My leetle VeekTOHRR."* (My little Victor.)

●Later in his life, Gideon drank heavily and lost their small hardscrabble farm while gambling. He separated from Lena and family, and for a while, ran a corner rural bar outside of Rice Lake. One of his local creditors, a personal enemy, angrily came into the bar one night. Gideon chased him out with a shotgun loaded with rock salt, shooting the man as he ran across the property line to get off the premises, as Gideon had ordered him. When it all went to court, the judge asked Gideon "Did you shoot him in defense?" Gideon responded in his heavily French-Canadian influenced English, "'ell no! I shot 'im da ass, as 'e went *over* da fence."

●Logging camp ways persist. Gideon poured grease from fried bacon or sausage onto his pancakes and bread for extra energy before hard, long days logging in the winter forest. My dad did that, and I confess to it myself, especially on cold, early camp mornings.

●Strong tea (not coffee), then a stimulant kept hot on the logging-camp fire all day, is still part of our lives here. The "camp boys" drank strong tea because it was cheaper, easier to make, and more available than coffee in the winter woods of those days, our older logger family members said.

●Gideon's few photographs show him as a handsome, fit, poised man, dressed well for the times and circumstances. His confidence, intelligence, and entrepreneur's heart are evident in his pictures.

Nowadays, as we hike the many trails here, we remember Grandpa Gideon's hiking heritage left to our family. We don't know if Gideon or his father Antoine Roi, both here as loggers from St. Alphonse, ever set foot directly on this land. But we know they came to northern Wisconsin for opportunities in the skilled, dangerous work they already knew well from their experience in the forests of eastern Canada. Once in northern Wisconsin, they likely worked on the St. Croix and Namekagon Rivers. Who knows, they may have spent time here at this high lake bank on the St. Croix, in this forest where we live.

In view of Grandpa Gideon's walks, our thousand miles per year in piece-meal chunks of about three miles a day on the North Country Trail, lake ice, and other forest and lake paths seem unimpressive. We know of other Native walkers, pioneer mail carriers, and area northlanders from the last centuries who also hiked and sledded with purpose to get around this still-wild area before roads and rails. Nonetheless, in our simple incremental way, we are pleased, step by step, to follow their tradition of perseverance and tenacity, enjoying the beauty and challenges of every season, as we explore out from our home near the Red Pump.

Ramblings on Our Rocks

Large glacial rocks, that is. Numerous beach-ball to Subaru-sized boulders lie randomly around our property. All are "glacial erratics", dropped by the half-mile-thick melting glaciers in this area as the last ice age ended around 10,000 years ago. These massive boulders are not likely to move, but think of the stories they could tell of their travels down the North American continent from northern Canadian Laurentian Shield country. Prior to our coming to rest here, our own ramblings, north to Canada then back here, resemble those of the rocks in ways.

One of the largest rock erratics on our land is right outside our front window, about 60 feet from the Red Pump; just a few steps beyond our home's lower-level south corner. I am looking at this biggest boulder now, as I write and stretch for a break to warm up a bit; outside air temperatures are at 32 degrees below zero Fahrenheit again this clear, bright January day. But, although it has been cold lately, I doubt the glaciers will be back, for a long while, at least. These rocks are not going to move.

We sometimes call this front yard boulder our "reunion rock" because of the names painted on it in the last century, and especially during early 1950s family reunion campfires and cookouts. You can still see names and initials of Favell and King family members affixed to it in fading black enamel paint. Years of weathering and lichen growth have obliterated or covered many of the inscriptions, but you can make out some of them: *TRF*, *Barb*, *Chris*, *Judy*, *EJF*, and others, all Favell folks; *Vic*, *Karen*, *Maddy*, and *Tommy*, the Kings. The rock is a solid reminder of the human history here; people we have loved and shared fun Solon Springs days with, some here 130 years ago.

To my knowledge, reunion rock has been moved twice by humans. The first time was by bulldozer when it was pushed about 50 feet north in the original small pasture, barn, and campsite clearing here around 1950, when my folks and Grandpa Favell (*EJF* on the rock) stewarded this land. It was moved the second time, as I watched, on June 26, 2002. Scott, our power shovel operator that day, nudged it inches at a time with his "bucket", south and west, just a short way from where glaciers had left it, so we could excavate for our house foundation. The rock will stay where it is now.

Other than those short moves, reunion rock competed its glacial ramblings here thousands of years ago. It has since been atop this pristine hundred-foot-deep glacial ground moraine of sand, gravel, and boulders, from which we draw our water and life. The giant rock, three tons at least, we're told, sets a clear example for us now: Stay here, near the Red Pump. This is the best place to be.

We had to make some careful, responsible, permanent decisions about this place in 2002, as we implemented our plans to build and live here. We tried to be entirely circumspect, and so gently slid reunion rock and a few other large ones in order to dig our full basement and build our simple, efficient home. Around 1970, I had studied an article in an issue of the then-new magazine, *The Mother Earth News* (the first ten years of which are still stored in our barn), on basic design for a passive-solar-assisted, earth-bermed home they named "Sunny Cave". It seemed relatively easy to build, and largely heated and cooled itself, to a point. Mainly, it held a fairly stable background temperature.

The principles of simple passive solar/earth-insulated home construction were laid out well in the article, and stuck in my memory all these years. I recalled them in our 2001-2002 planning, with the main points being: 1. Build your small, extremely well-insulated house with a full below ground basement as the lower floor. 2. Use large, energy-efficient windows on the south and east sides, with south windows aimed into the noon mid-January sun. 3. Backfill with earth to the bottom of the siding near the above-grade floor level.

The idea is proving itself. We have created a "thermos bottle with windows" pointed south which, in cold seasons, gains heat from the sun and retains background earth warmth. In warmer seasons, our home stays cool for the same reasons, with the addition of insulated sun-blocking blinds on all windows and doors to minimize heat entry during the day for summer, and to keep heat in during winter. Earth temperature here is about 40-45 degrees F year around, certainly not warm by most standards, but much warmer than the 30 below outside today, and definitely well above freezing. We warm the house up or cool it down from this more stable central temperature, rather than from outside extremes. Life in the sandy forests of Solon Springs during a year can be lived at outside temperatures ranging from 30-40 degrees below zero, plus wind-chill factors to 50 below or lower, to 100 degrees or more above zero in summer: quite a challenging span for engineering a passive, self-maintaining home. We are finding our simple, effective design works reasonably well, even without supplementary sources of heating or cooling. The house essentially takes care of itself. Most importantly, it is protected from freezing up inside, even if we are gone for days at a time or electricity goes out.

Importantly, to augment the basic design, we installed thick, state-of-the-art thermal waffle blinds, "bottom-up/top-down" types, on all east and south windows and doors, and kept all other windows and doors to a minimum on west and north sides. We also installed back-up electric baseboard heating units in each individual room, downstairs and up, to help out on extremely cold days, like today. This is especially functional and efficient because you can boost heat in just the room you are in, then turn it up, down, or fully off, as you wish. Further, we wired in large, well-anchored reversible ceiling fans upstairs, and use smaller, safe room fans, upstairs and down, to aid air movement, heating, and cooling as needed.

Our simple passive design works and makes a great home. *Sunny Cove* here is actually our second iteration of this "Mother Earth" home we have built, with our first on a little city lot in Superior. In that home, we relied on a centrally positioned woodstove downstairs to heat the whole house, so we seldom needed the electrical back-up units. Our current home is better built and more heavily insulated, with some of our walls a foot or more thick, with "R" insulation ratings of 40 plus, and our super-insulated upper-floor ceiling at R factors of 52 plus. Chronic asthma is part of our family story now, so we have avoided burning wood inside.

Originally, we built our home this way because we knew we would be gone from it often, sometimes for lengthy periods; it would need to sustain itself. If a furnace fans breaks, or a gas line malfunctions, we knew we may not be immediately available to handle to repair, and in this climate, that can be disastrous. Oil or gas heat sources were out. Here in the country, where we may be absent for long times with travels or work, and have no one near who can check the place easily for us, and where furnace repairs and maintenance are less easy to schedule, we have found our hands-off, passive solar and earth design works as planned.

Our trial runs here have shown that in extremely cold weather, the house coasts back to background temperature of about 48-50 degrees, not warm, but certainly way warmer than 30 below, and well above the danger point for our pipes freezing. In hot summer weeks, we find the ground level floor of the house will get to about 78-82 degrees maximum if left alone. The lower below-grade level stays a pretty constant 73-76 degrees, even during periods of 100-plus degree heat outside. We use our fans or heaters to help adjust the temperature and comfort levels up or down, depending on the season and weather, but are pleased that we can be this self-contained. Being warm enough and cool enough are central to all the rest of life here. That reliable background, isothermal temperature of earth assures us our house should never freeze up, even if we are gone for an extended time. We trust that reamins true.

At the core of our home and small barn were the ideas of respecting our land, and not clearing any more than absolutely necessary. Our house and barn size were governed by the radius of turns in our winding access road from the south. We were determined and successful in keeping everything small and tight enough that NO trees, especially our big Norway and white pines, were dinged or harmed in snaking in and out all of our equipment and materials. Forest impact was minimal

As everything had to roll on forest soil that had not been disturbed in more than a hundred years, if ever, we wanted to keep the impact, the literal footprint, of all we brought in and out to a respectful minimum for our ground and vegetation. It again seemed to work. We built this compact, self-regulating house, and a small barn, which contain our studios, storage attic, two-car garage, and the "Sheltie Shack" small kennel for our brother and sister dogs, Scotty and Sonja. We kid that life here must be like living on the International Space Station because everything is state-of-the-art new and efficient, but compact. Sometimes here, it feels like we are camping out every day. It takes some learning and getting along to make it work daily, but so far so good.

This clearing where we live has been the site of at least four small house trailers, as I recall, that my parents and we parked here over the years in our camping spot. We moved in and leveled up a new pre-built, ornate tool shed in 2000, bought from a local builder with funds my dad had given us years before. We placed it as a remembrance of him, and it is doing well. A very useful, well-filled shed that serves as a daily reminder of Voyageur Victor and all our days here before and with the Red Pump, which he so carefully placed on our well.

We also have built all-poplar pole outhouses, various small tool sheds, an eight-by-sixteen-foot steel pole building that covered the Red Pump, and many camp tables, swings, and other minor pioneering aids for rustic living on this land in days before our building spree. Thomas and Angela Favell had built a small barn just to the south of our home now for their two cows. It is mentioned in Angela's story "A Smart Dog" earlier in this book. That barn burned from a lightning strike around 1923, and the charred cedar and pine logs of it, as well as the original south barbed-wire fence line from the property boundary of the late 1880s, are still lying in the ground. Though a neighbor pulled up and threw away much of the barbed wire, we leave the rest as a marker of where the property begins and ends, and a record of human life here in days before our arrival. Local history tells that this was an Ojibwa camping area for hundreds or years, but we have not found evidence of that yet on this parcel. A few years ago, we built a one-kilometer (0.6 mile) trail through our forest, to help explore what lies here. We hike, ski, snowshoe, and/or walk the dogs on it all days possible, with discoveries of past life here yet to happen, I'm sure.

Before the Red Pump, our first water well here was a driven "sand point", positioned below our front bank near the road on our east side, toward Lake St. Croix. Dad and I drove it with just the point, a few lengths of pipe, and a large hammer in 1958. It went down a total of 23 feet, and gushed artesian water for years. The water always tested pure in all our samples sent to state labs in Madison at that time. With the vertical T-pipe and elbow on the constantly-gushing well head, it made a convenient drinking fountain: just cover the lower part of the T with your hand, and the water burbled up six inches or more, great for drinking. It sure attracted all the neighbor kids. The well water ran all year round, and was till running fine when Dad and I pulled in out in the summer of 1973, after we had drilled and hooked up the Red Pump up above on our camping area on the hill.

My own ramblings took me north into Ontario for a while, and then back here to northwestern Wisconsin. When Debbi and I first moved back to this true Badger northland after our marriage in 1975, we almost built here at Solon Springs, but decided to build on a small lot we had bought in Superior. That was a great home, and a fine place to live, with convenient access to the university, schools, shopping, and all of the Twin Ports resources. We built the prototype of this house there, and now I am glad we waited to build here. We did it right, we think, and felt we had to *the first time* on this precious, cherished ground. We have tried to make no major mistakes in our designs and buildings here, keeping everything as simple, sustainable, and waste-free as possible for our budget and skills. We hope that proves out forever more, and for future generations of ours who will live here. It is good that we rambled back to take up our permanent home, just like our solid, big rocks.

Kingswood Rock Fest 2007, or Boulder Mania, as son Seth called it, hit us in August and September of that year; it seemed to strike Debbi and me at the same time. We had walked by and looked over our many rocks for all these years, and said one day "Let's move 'em!" Debbi still covets boulders of others' we see around the neighborhood, but I think our boulder moving days are over. We hired a skid-steer and operator to move the bigger ones, and we moved around a hundred of our own volley ball to garbage can sized boulders ourselves, by hand, careful rolling, and sliding and lifting with ropes, pulleys, and levers. We were *so* careful to not get near to or damage any of the Red Pump area or our buildings. We did it; all went well, and our Rock Fest work got us in great shape. It was fun but a lot of work, and we are done.

Our rambling days are over, and so, too, the ramblings of our rocks. Sometimes it is just best to know when you are home and stable in life, and that you can stop moving. For our glacial erratics, the rambling rocks, and for us, that is now true. We hope it will be so for all our days here at Sunny Cove. Home at last, the rocks and us. Rambling no more.

Donut Dog Dumps Canoe

Ice had left the lake a few days earlier, and the Upper St. Croix River, flowing south to Gordon and beyond, was an inviting three-hour canoe trip for our families. Four adults, three boys, one dog, and one bag of fresh bakery donuts, all out for an early April canoe trip on the St. Croix. So how was it that two humans and dog were soon swimming for shore?

Canoeists getting wet, especially in water that was ice a day or two before, is not a good thing. Here's how it happened. Our friends, Len and Betsy, with their younger son Jeff, were back at the lake's western "Cozy Cove" shore, getting settled in their canoe and stowing gear they would need on our trip. We were all experienced canoeists, and excited to explore the open, clear river.

Seth and I, along with Shiku, our thirty-pound American Eskimo female dog, had already paddled ahead to get on the lake and out of the way of the others. We stopped and waited while Adam and Debbi packed their canoe. They launched, then paddled out to join us. As Adam and Debbi approached us, they asked if we could toss the donut bag to them. We positioned our boats about six feet apart and got ready. I lobbed the tightly closed white bakery bag with recently warm donuts so it would arc and land in their canoe. That's when Shiku jumped for the moving bag. We hadn't planned on that. She leaned hard against our left gunwale at about the center thwart, toward Adam's boat, nearly swamping Seth and me. Adam reached out quickly for the donuts; the bag was now far off my intended trajectory. He and Debbi tried to balance and compensate for that sharp rocking disturbance in their equilibrium, but they could not. They went over–instantly. It happened in an eye blink. I can still see the slow-motion movie in my mind.

As you can imagine, they gasped, splashing and thrashing in the cold water. We could see the surprised fear in Shiku's eyes as she surfaced, a sleek, soaked, wet-rat dog; so skinny, so scared. She dog-paddled to the shore a few yards away, shook off, and watched her humans perform. Debbi and Adam kept their composure and swam for shallow water. My shouting "She's gonna die!" toward my water-wary wife may not have been all that appropriate. She was fine. Adam and Debbi simply swam a few strokes toward shore, got into waist deep water, and found firm bottom to stand on. They easily walked in to the grassy lake bank. Shiku, content and mostly dried by now, sniffed around on the shore, probably still thinking about those donuts.

To everyone's good fortune, the day was sunny, with a strong, warm south breeze. We retrieved the flipped canoe and pulled it in. Our boys and I lifted and drained it, setting it upright, gently beached on the gravel bottom near shore. Debbi and Adam rang out their clothes and socks, and recovered all but one shoe. We were happy, laughing, and ready again in minutes.

Through all this, our friends were back at Cozy Cove, still getting set. Their attention was diverted from the festivities we were providing on the lake, out of hearing range from them. We had just drained the canoe and were drying off on the turf bank when they paddled up close enough to see the aftermath. They registered little surprise as they got closer to us, saying that it appeared to them as normal for the Kings, activities they expected of us: a quick cold-water dip and canoe swamping, parts of our annual spring rituals, they assumed.

Humans and canine were warmed and willing, so we headed down river, expecting our usual lazy trip. This day, however, headwinds from the southwest were fierce, with our "easy paddle" taking hours of hard stroking to, at last, dock at the Gordon ranger station. We gained insights that long day into why Native and European voyageurs, traders and explorers poled their way *up* this part of the river, often in low, flat-bottomed bateaus. Going upstream against flowing water currents would have been *way* less work, we figured, than bucking the warm but hard, pernicious spring winds our whole trip. Overall, family lessons of resilience were learned that day, with great memories also of Len, Betsy, and Jeff, our tolerant, good friends.

By the way, the donuts and bag sank. We never found them.

Toasted Science

Cooking on the campfire here near the Red Pump is always a joy, and more fun than a guy should be able to have with his hiking boots on. In fact, I'm a much better cook with an outdoor hardwood fire than over an indoor stove. Breakfasts are my favorite, followed by deep-dish Dutch oven delectables made on thick bed of glowing coals.

We aging scientists, educators, and breakfast cooks know there are certain central scientific principles that have come to permeate our cooking, and our lives, recreation, and professional disciplines. Ohm's Law, gravitational theory, the heliocentric solar system, and many other observation-based principles guide our thinking, and may even help us make a better omelet. But there are other immutable laws of existence we don't know much about.

Important findings about one such universal principle and the work of dedicated British researchers were recently summarized in science journals and on the web. After engaging more than a thousand school children and their teachers in the project, and after conducting over 20,000 objective closely-controlled and observed experimental events, investigators determined: The buttered side of toast indeed lands face-down about 62% of the time, when dropped to the floor from a standardized height. So, about two-thirds of the time, we can count on our floor-flopped toast landing buttered side down. It sure seems like every time to me. Maybe we should just butter the other side?

Here's another principle for immediate further investigation: When you are canoeing or kayaking, especially on large open bodies of water, the wind will always come directly at you so that you will always paddle against the wind. In my observations, if you rotate your canoe 180 degrees (that is, turn around and go the other way), the wind will immediately reverse direction and still come directly at you, head on. If you reverse direction yet again, this will continue to be true, and so on. The wind knows. It conspires against your forward motion and wants to make you paddle harder. I have no firm data on this, but repeated sampling events over many years and miles of canoeing have made me a believer.

Other research areas in which junior, tenure-track faculty members might secure large foundation grants include: The Shirt-Label-Rotation Phenomenon (SLRP). Specifically: Why is it that whichever way you place your T-shirt or sweatshirt on the bed or dresser, the shirt will always be rotated backwards when you next go to put it on? In other words, the label will always be in front, and you will have to turn the shirt over or around so you don't put it on backwards. It always happens. Even if you carefully put your shirt down so that the label will be correctly placed when you return to put on your shirt, it will still be the wrong way. The label obviously changes locations. This must be an unreported nuance of quantum physics, probably related to the Heisenberg Uncertainty Principle.

The universe offers us other, even more puzzling phenomena to study. For example, The Running-Out-of-Staples-in-Your-Staple-Gun-as-Soon-as-You-Wriggle-Your-Way-to-the-Top-of-the-Ladder-and-Get-into-Position-to-Staple-Those-High-and-Difficult-Pieces-of-Insulation-up-in-the-Tight-Corner Effect. Why do you always run out of staples only then? The same thing applies in painting walls and ceilings: The brush or roller won't drip on the floor, or be out of paint, until you get to the very top of your ladder and squirm into position to start painting that tough, high corner.

These issues intrigue me. I could describe many other topics for indoor and outdoor applied and basic research, but you must excuse me: my campfire toast is getting cold.

Paradise Lost...and Found

Wausau seemed a long way from our northland paradise, Solon Springs, as our village-in-the-forest disappeared in my rearview mirror. My Wisconsin Regional Writers' Association registration was sent in August, and I immediately put the September 2008 conference on my calendar. Going, at last, indeed. I'd heard of this curious WRWA event many times over the past few years from other writers in northern Wisconsin. Even more curiously: although I was raised by and among writers, and although I have spent a lifetime writing, and although I have lived in southern, central, and true northern Wisconsin over many years, and although I have been connected with at least twelve of the state's university and college campuses as student, staff, faculty, and/or parent, *I had never even known of WRWA,* until winter 2002. Joining the smart, active St. Croix Writers' Group here in little but so literate Solon Springs changed that.

When I pulled into the hotel in Wausau that Friday afternoon, my first thoughts were that was a long drive, but worth it to get to this truly geographically central place in the state. As I checked into my room, looked around the hotel, read a local paper, watched the news a bit, and spoke with others, I was struck by how insular and cloistered this area of the state seemed to me now. At home here in the Twin Ports area, we are accustomed to Canadian flags, money, and license plates, as well as U of M and Minnesota Vikings signs, bumper stickers, shirts, and news, in addition, of course, to full Badger, Packer, and general Wisconsin coverage we get in our northwestern part of the state via all means of print and electronic media. This was a bit of culture shock for me, and frankly, a good learning experience from the beginning of my stay. It had been years since I spent a couple of days immersed in central Wisconsin, not just passing through on the highway or overhead on a flight to Milwaukee or Toronto.

My first WRWA conference, the groups' 60th, was truly a literary, social, and intellectual treat. Informal chats and greeting times allowed me to engage with many writers from around the state. Our younger son, physicist Seth, and Katie, his English-teacher girl friend, even drove up from the Milwaukee area to spend a few hours with me in Wausau and have dinner on Friday night. They accompanied me to the evening poetry and prose reading sessions, and enjoyed them. I read one of my new performance pieces, "(w)Riters' (w)Rap", from one of my upcoming books and new CDs. They all seemed to like it, and the prose group heard two short chapters from another of my current print and audio book projects, *Tales from the Red Pump*. What a pleasure to share. I enjoyed and learned a lot from the other readers' works, and from their feedback on mine in both sessions that night. It felt good to contribute some new work, perhaps a varying perspective for new friends in these groups.

Saturday's opening program at the conference was memorable. They asked me to do "the rap" one more time for the large group; all seemed to like it. I was honored to be asked. Also then, as sometimes occurs in our lives, serendipity stepped in. I could not have planned it.

Conference organizers introduced me to the daughter of WRWA founder Robert Gard. Before her presentation began, Maryo Gard Ewell and I talked of our own families, and had a wonderful discussion about her father's work, rural Wisconsin, and stories of life in our state through many decades of writers. She and others recruited me to help read a short play, which I believe she had specially written to commemorate this amazing 60th anniversary of her father's founding of our (now *my*) writing association in Wisconsin. They gave me a copy of the many pages with our parts, and I did my best to cold-read along in front of the large meeting, filling in my lines as the "yellow-highlighter guy" role with other readers. What a simple but effective, historic engagement for us all at this once-in-our-lifetimes event. Sixty years, wow. None of us there will see the doubling of that anniversary. Once again, I learned much, and was pleased to have a small part in this major anniversary of the group. Although I was truly a walk-on, a total newbie to the group, it was great to be included. Thanks WRWA folks.

As we read through our play, and as I reflected on it afterward, the extent of my good fortune at being involved further struck me. Ms. Gard Ewell's family and mine shared interests and activities from that time 60 or more years ago. We also shared common history, as it pertains to telling the story of Wisconsin, often from these more rural areas. Her father, Robert, so interested in and dedicated to literacy, was a professor at UW-Madison in those years. My great uncle, Clough Gates, of Superior, dedicated to education and literacy in the northland and the whole state, was a University of Wisconsin Regent, and was managing editor of the Superior Evening Telegram newspaper from earlier twentieth-century years, into the 1960s. When I was a young boy, he told me of the long train ride, or 10-hour-plus one-way drive to Madison in the early 1900s, often on gravel and two-lane roads, earlier versions of Wisconsin Highways 53 and 12, through all the small towns of southern Wisconsin it seemed. Remember: Interstate Highway 94 was not connected from the Eau Claire area to Madison until the late 1960s, and Highway 53, Eau Claire to Superior, just became fully-open four lane expressway in the past few years, with easy connection now through to I- 94 south and east. If only he'd had those roads then.

Uncle Clough described to me, but never complained about, how long it took to travel to and from Madison for his many meetings each year as a Regent. He also had season UW football tickets for Camp Randall Stadium, where he and our family went to UW games together in the 1950s and 1960s. Maryo Gard Ewell's detailed WRWA play that we read to the conference audience about Professor Gard mentions UW President Frank and other University leaders of that time. Some of Clough Gates' writings from that period, still archived at the Wisconsin Historical Society and in our files here, tell of stories and history of Superior and Douglas County. Some of his works also speak of these same UW notables, and Regent Gates' many strong reactions to UW policies and procedures of that era.

Intriguingly, Professor Gard and Regent/Editor Gates, Maryo's and my revered relatives, likely crossed paths in Mecca Madison of that time: at the Memorial Union, on Bascom Hill, or perhaps in their trips around the state at other sites of literary interest to them both. Whether at their headquarters, in Superior or in Madison, or around the state in their travels, both sought, collected, wrote, and edited some of the stories of Wisconsin's diverse, tough, innovative people during those years. I wonder if they knew each other, or ever collaborated? Maybe they were friends? It is a small world.

As Maryo told of Robert Gard's writing and producing of numerous plays and skits for Wisconsin Public radio in her and my growing-up years of the 1950s and 1960s, I chuckled knowingly. My parents, sister, and I daily listened to what they called at that time the "state educational radio network" as we lived in various parts of Wisconsin. I'm certain we heard works of Robert Gard's, but I never connected that with a real man and family, until we read the play at WRWA. What a privilege.

I also inwardly chuckled a bit when one of the helpers at the registration desk asserted this year's attendance at the conference was down because, paraphrasing, "Wausau was a long way for writers from Madison and Milwaukee to travel." The helper asserted that the conference should be held in a more central location for them. As I thought of Uncle Clough Gates, a 1902 journalism and business graduate of UW-Madison, and his many years of trekking in all seasons from Superior to Madison and back regularly, on rugged gravel and two-lane back roads even into the 1950s and 1960s, I smiled at the comment. If only that helper knew of the miles and hours of travel put in by so many Wisconsin folks like Gard and Gates, and the stories we all likely have.

Robert Gard and Clough Gates *knew* rural Wisconsin travel well, as a lot of us Badgers do. We in the rural north accept that, sometimes, we must travel from our northwestern Paradise to do important things nearer southern Wisconsin population centers. And then we get to return here, thank goodness! Just think of the stories and lessons so many of us can tell of lives up, down, and around this state. Robert Gard helped bring those stories and memories to us through writings, and catalyzed a lasting process for sharing them. WRWA provides another way all of us can share this important work, preserving our varied stories of diverse, wonderful Wisconsin. We write, we rite, we right!

Red Pump Backstory and Cast

Many personalities are featured in these *Tales from the Red Pump*. Our true central character throughout, the Red Pump, has quite a story itself. The Red Pump serves as our limnological and literary hub of human and natural history of this place, and of these Tales. It is a newcomer to this ancient forest and clearing, part of family land since around 1890. As with all other players in these small tales, parts of real daily history of the Northland, the pump also has humble origins.

Victor, my father, and always the preeminent scrounger and bargainer, located the pump at a second-hand and surplus store south of Superior, Wisconsin. Dad bought it for five dollars in spring, 1973, and carted it here in the trunk of his 1972 Dodge Dart, his favorite car which he used daily in his work travels for the state. Lettering on the pump's embossed, cast-iron pressure chamber still clearly reads: Superior Duplex Manufacturing Company 1905. We learned the Duplex Company was a leading maker of pumps in this region at that time, and we see our pump's relatives still in place and probably working at many rural homes and farms around northland Wisconsin.

The pump was a worn-out, scratched, faded barn-red color when Dad bought it, but he soon painted it silver that early spring, 1973, to protect it from rust. Dad and I mounted it on our new water well after it was drilled that spring by Mr. R. Lind and his Lind Well Drilling Company of Iron River, Wisconsin. Mr. Lind and crew bored 126 feet into sand, gravel, boulders, then deep bedrock in our forest clearing, and we have had pure, clear, cold (42 degree F) water ever since. Our state and county health department water tests over the years have always shown maximum purity, with water starting at about 29 feet down from the ground surface.

The well was constructed so it would drain back and hold residual water down at about eight feet from the well top. This required just three pump strokes on the long, lever handle to bring water up, year around. Mr. Lind wisely configured the pump with a subterranean drain hole, so it would never freeze up, and would be usable in all weather. The Duplex Pump even has a machined hose fitting and pressurizing feature for pumping water by hand over long distances on the farm. We never utilized that application, but knew it was good to have, especially if fire ever threatened our woods.

The well and our then *silver* pump were quickly the functioning, beating heart of our land and our forest lives here. For us, it became forever more "The Red Pump" several years later when we repainted our cherished new-old friend a bright, glossy, rustproof red, top to bottom. When we built our home here in 2002, we unbolted the Red Pump, and hooked in an electric well pump to supply water for the house. The Red Pump has been carefully moved and mounted in a rock garden, just a few steps from where it performed so reliably from 1973 into 2002. It is the honored center of our front yard clearing now, a shrine of sorts to simplicity and our satisfying life in the northland woods. (Check the front cover to see how the Red Pump is doing as of summer 2008.)

The larger story here, prior to the Red Pump, began for our family in this village about 120 years ago. In 1896, the water bottling and shipping business started by Mr. T. F. Solon lent its name, at least informally for many, to this frequent railroad stop, Solon Springs. That new name, adopted from the sign on the railroad siding for the bottling plant just south of us, replaced in common parlance, the previous village name, White Birch, as it was called by Native peoples, in their languages. Official Solon Springs paperwork for name change was not filed until the 1920s, we have been told. The facts are not yet clear.

Prior to this, my great grandparents, Thomas and Angela Favell, homesteaded property east and then west of White Birch/Solon Springs around 1886 through the 1890s to early 1900s. Along with Mr. Solon, Thomas Favell conducted some of the original surveying on the south, Spring Hill Addition portion of Solon Spring in the late 1890s through 1904. Thomas, my great grandfather, was a Civil War veteran, a war hero many said of him, who, though never severely wounded, suffered difficult bouts with malaria during his four full years of active, dangerous service in battle on the front lines. He served, with and was lay chaplain for, the Wisconsin 8th, the Eagle Regiment, who carried their famous mascot "Old Abe" into combat. Thomas wrote that he never saw a man fall from his own gun in the four years he served, although he fought in numerous fierce, deadly skirmishes. His collected letters and hand-written first-person accounts of the 8th Regiment and his four years in the Civil War are part of family archives. The transcribed, bound copy of his writings, *Civil War Years,* is available at the Wisconsin Historical Society Library. Please see Red Pump References for more details.

Thomas' wife, Angela Haste Favell, my great grandmother, was an active, literate, visionary Wisconsin pioneer woman from the state's early days. Angela had a deep, life-long interest in learning, creating, inventing, and making her own strong way in life. She later became an author known now throughout Wisconsin for her recounting of her pioneer life and her family's homesteading days in several parts of the state. The homestead property we live on now was her third of her long life of nearly 103 years. She and Thomas came here to the Upper St. Croix Lake basin, homesteading "Shore Acres" their lake and farm home, which also originally included a ten-acre forest and pasture farm tract. She mentions these in her piece "A Smart Dog" included earlier in this book. Some of her reminiscences of pioneer homesteading in Wisconsin are posted at the Wisconsin Historical Society web site, *Turning Points*, and have also become part of the Wisconsin secondary school history curriculum. Please see Red Pump References for details.

The Favell and King families have had full lives and adventures emanating from this property for at least 130 years. Thomas' and Angela's son, Earnest John Favell, my grandfather, loved this land. He and his wife, Inga Maria (Olsen) Favell, my grandmother, lived and recreated on it more than a hundred years ago, and then passed it on to the next generation. Victor and Madeline (Favell) King, my parents, and Clough Gates and his wife Mabel (Favell) Gates (Thomas' and Angela's daughter), also stewarded this very property for years. All of these family members felt the power and attraction of the Upper Lake St. Croix basin in their long lives.

Early in our lives together, my wife, our sons, and I all re-learned the special, visceral draw of these lands and waters from our family's many years of life, challenges, and adventures here. We continue those adventures daily, appreciating this unique place more fully as we all grow older and wiser. We will always have much more to tell of growing and living in the Northland, this wonderful Wisconsin paradise.

144

The Cast

Tales from the Red Pump

The Favell Family:

Thomas & Angela (Haste) and Ernest & Inga Maria (Olsen)

The Gates Family:

Clough & Mabel (Favell)

The King Family:

Antoine Roi.   Gideon Roi & Magdalena (Hetzenekkar)

Victor & Madeline (Favell) & Karen

Thomas & Debra (Torgerson) & Adam & Seth

~ Adam married Lindsey Rae (Chamberlain) King in 2004.
She and their growing family will be part of upcoming
More Tales from the Red Pump. ~

Red Pump References and Resources

Favell, Gates, and King family members have been and are recognized writers. Some of our family's pioneer history and written works, as well as other life information and career background, are available as follows:

Angela Haste Favell, an early Wisconsin pioneer homesteader and settler in Solon Springs, Superior, Waupaca, and Royalton areas, was my great grandmother. We reside on forestland that was part of her and husband Thomas' post-civil-war homestead (her third in her long life of 102 years) here in Solon Springs, WI. Some of her writings, circa 1932, are at WHS Turning Points site and are used in Wisconsin secondary school history curricula, particularly her work, *A Girl Pioneer in the Wisconsin Wilderness,* Angela's personal memoir of her family's early homesteading experiences and adventures in Wisconsin forests of the era. Her original article, both the handwritten and typed, self-bound versions, are on file here in our archives as well as in the Wisconsin Historical Society Library. The *Milwaukee Journal* scanned version is at:

http://www.wisconsinhistory.org/turningpoints/search.asp?id=954

Angela's *The Story of Old Abe* (eagle mascot of the Wisconsin 8th Regiment in the Civil War) was assembled, edited, and self-published by her granddaughter, my mother, Madeline (Favell) King in 1976, the US bicentennial year. It and other information on Angela, her pioneer life, and family are also available via the WHS library archives.

Thomas Favell, husband of Angela Haste Favell, was my great grandfather and my namesake. *Civil War Years*, Thomas' collected original letters to family at home, date from his "mustering in" at Camp Randall, Madison, WI, 1861, on through the entire Civil War to his mustering out, again at Camp Randal, 1865. His hand-written letters were assembled, transcribed, and narrated by his grandson and great granddaughter, Thomas R. Favell and Judith Favell in 1976.

Clough Gates, early Superior resident, my great uncle, Editor of *Superior Evening Telegram* for years, and University of Wisconsin (Madison) Regent in the1930s, wrote several works still archived and available at the Wisconsin Historical Society library. Some publications include: *Superior: an outline of history - July 15, 1954,* a summary of Douglas County and Superior history, in Superior Centennial year, 1954. He also published *Statements relative to: 1. The Presidency of the University of Wisconsin and its relationship to the Board of Regents, 2. Certain claims of President Frank concerning the Progress of the University of Wisconsin under his Leadership. January 6-7, 1937.*

Thomas and Debra King recall some of their alumni memories from years as students, staff, and faculty at the University of Wisconsin- Eau Claire at: **http://www.uwec.edu/alumni/bliss/king.htm**. Thomas Wayne King has written and published textbooks, books, chapters, articles, essays, poems, instrumental and vocal compositions, and song recordings of all types. He is Professor Emeritus, UWEC. Debra Raye King is Dean of Students at Wisconsin Indianhead Technical College-Superior. They and their immediate family have many University of Wisconsin System degrees and experiences spanning six decades. Debra's life is further detailed in *The Woman Today* magazine, February/March 2009 issue, at **www.thewomantoday.com** pages 70-71.

Red Pump Timeline

Days flow quickly into next days; years into next years. A compressed time panorama gives perspective for our Tales and cast. Whether we regard time as a circle or line, a time scale reminds us that things change. Ultimately, change is our only certainty. Focal dates listed in this abridged scale are a just few of many other important events we note in our forest home near the Red Pump:

12,000-10,000 years BCE: Wisconsin glacial period ends. St. Croix Lake and river valley formed. Paleo-Indians thrive in this rich region of lakes & forests.

Circa 1600-1700: Ojibwa people arrive; Lakota/Sioux here. Europeans travel through and explore area: Sieur DuLhut, Marquette, many others.

Early-Mid 1800s: Village called White Birch, from original Native name. Area also becoming of interest to railroad, logging, and other businesses.

1838: Thomas Favell born, St. Louis Co., NY; moves to Royalton/Waupaca, WI area as child. Literate farmer, lumberman, businessman, pioneer settler.

1851: Angela Haste born, Fox Lake, IL; family soon homesteads in Waupaca, WI area. She later writes of Wisconsin pioneer life & her homesteading family.

1861-1865: American Civil War. Thomas Favell, 8th WI (Eagle) Regiment; war hero of sorts, serves all four years, mustered in/out, Madison, Wisconsin.

1867: Thomas & Angela married November 1867, Royalton, WI; lumbering, farming, other businesses. Move to Missouri to farm. Children born there.

1870: Ernest J. Favell born May 17; Mabel Favell born 1876; survivors of 4 children, to Thomas & Angela. Family soon returns from MO to settle in WI.

Circa 1880: Gideon Roi (King) to WI from Quebec; father, Antoine, follows. Ennar Edward & Christina (Moe) Olsen, to Hayward, WI from Oslo, Norway.

1886-91: Thomas & Angela & family prepare to leave Royalton, WI, for booming Superior area. They first travel through & visit White Birch village.

1886: Inga Maria Olsen born, Hayward; baptized, Lutheran Ch.; family move, Duluth. Orchestra pianist/mandolinist. Duluth Central HS; DBC grad, c. 1902.

1888: Gideon marries Magdalena Hetzenekkar, Hayward, WI. They operate 'Stopping Place' restaurant/bar; continue farming, logging; have 7 children.

Circa 1896: White Birch called 'Solon Springs' for Mr. T. Solon, founder of spring water bottling plant; village takes name of railroad siding sign for plant.

1901-02: Thomas & Angela Favell homestead west of lake, 10 + acres; build 'Shore Acres' farm/lake home & 7 'Favell Cottages' on west side; all still in SS.

1902: Ernest John Favell, Ripon College graduate, earns DO medical degree at Kirksville, MO, College of Osteopathy. Licensed as physician in Wisconsin.

1905: The Red Pump produced in Superior, WI by Duplex Manufacturing Company. Duplex becomes a popular, much-used pump in this rural region.

1909: Dr. Ernest John Favell, DO, & Inga Maria Olsen married, Portland, OR. Celebration also held at Shore Acres, Solon Springs; live at Piney Ridge, SS.

1908: Victor Henry King born on rural Rice Lake, WI, farm. He is last child of seven; only one born in wood-frame house; not tent, cabin, covered wagon.

1911: Madeline Ramona Favell (King) born at home, Banks Ave., Superior. Rice Lake HS grad; B. S. Ed. degree, Superior State, 1933. Lives with Gates.

1918: Thomas Favell passes away, Superior. He was glad to learn Great War, WWI, war to end all wars, was over. Blind in his last years; glasses safe here.

1933: Victor & Madeline married, Chicago; Victor, U of Ill. pharmacy grad; RPh; works in/owns several southern WI stores; north to Menomonie, 1955-56.

1939: Karen Angela King born, Watertown, WI. World War II looming, troubled economy. Rationing soon a fact of life. Karen very ill at 18 months.

1950: Thomas Wayne King born, Walworth County, WI. First trip to 'Cozy Cove', summer 1950, with parents. Begins travels to, love of Superior/SS areas.

1950-51: Ernest John ('Doc') Favell builds, moves in, retires to his new Solon Springs log cabin, 'Cozy Cove' (aka *Cedar Cove*); southwestern shore, USCL.

1952: Inga Maria Olsen Favell, brilliant musician and businesswoman, passes on to compositions and composure yet undreamed. Chippewa Falls, WI.

1953: Angela Haste Favell passes away, Veterans Home, King, WI; writer, inventor, strong, creative pioneer; her WI writings are still vivid & compelling

1953: Debra Raye Torgerson (King) born, Menomonie. Kings making regular visits to Superior & Solon Springs; she joins their northland fun in 1974-75.

1956: Mabel Favell Gates deceased. Clough Gates passes on, 1965.

1967: Victor King names Kingswood. In 1968: VK & TK Isle Royale trips begin; many stops in Solon Springs. Need for good well and pump evident.

1973: Red Pump & deep water well installed at Kingswood, Solon Springs, in NE corner of campsite clearing. We build small metal shed; protects wellhead.

1975: Thomas & Debra married, move to Superior. We build our first small, efficient earth-friendly home, use wood heat; boys grow, thrive here; move '86.

1979: Adam born, Duluth, Minnesota. (BS, MS, biochem, UW-Madison, 2002; MD, Medical College of Wisconsin, 2006). Celebrations here/there.

1980: Seth born, Duluth, Minnesota. (BS, physics, UWEC; Ph. D., physics, UW-Milwaukee, 2009). Celebrations continue. What sons we have.

2000: Karen Angela King passes on, Hudson, WI. Brave, resolute, difficult life. A new, better swing awaits her; my hero, mentor, & my first, best teacher.

2002: We build home "Sunny Cove" at Kingswood, SS; begin our return to northland, so many years gone. Three years of construction to make livable.

2004: Debra, new Dean, WITC-Superior, moves to Solon Springs; we build studios/barn. Adam & Lindsey married. Sunny Cove work continues weekly.

2005: Thomas King retires, UWEC; moves to Solon Springs. Madeline Favell King passes on, June 3, Eau Claire. We owe our love of Solon Springs to her.

2005: Shiku Ukiuk leaves us. Scotty Boots & sister Molly Mitts born, July 28. We bring them here Sept. 30. Bright fall Puppy Days; fun transitions for T/D.

2006: *Tales* writing begins, Jan. 28. Molly killed Feb. 21. Sonja Socks born Feb.14. These were emotionally trying years for us; highs and lows abound.

2006: Sonja moves here, April 9. We get a chance at a do over. We all celebrate Adam's MD, as he begins medical career, Milwaukee, WI area.

2009: Seth gets Ph.D. Well-earned joy; new physics prof, UWLX. *Tales from the Red Pump* & *Lyrics*...published. *More Tales...*begins. New *Tales* cast await.

The small stories of our Northland paradise continue.

150

www.ingramcontent.com/pod-product-compliance
Lightning Source LLC
Chambersburg PA
CBHW051829040426

42447CB00006B/440